NO FEAR

Moving Mountains and Slaying Dragons

RICHARD BYLAND

CREATION HOUSE

A STRANG COMPANY

NO FEAR: MOVING MOUNTAINS AND SLAYING DRAGONS
by Richard Byland
Published by Creation House
A Strang Company
600 Rinehart Road
Lake Mary, Florida 32746
www.creationhouse.com

Unless otherwise noted, all Scripture quotations are from the King James Version of the Bible.

Cover design by Terry Clifton
Cover illustration by A.B. Duschane

Library of Congress Control Number: 2004117293
International Standard Book Number: 1-59185-785-6

05 06 07 08 09— 987654321
Printed in the United States of America

To all my friends along life's course whom I've let fall by the way.

CONTENTS

INTRODUCTION

THE APOSTLE JOHN was getting on in years when he received the Revelation of Jesus Christ on the island of Patmos. John was "the disciple whom Jesus loved" (John 21:20), and it was he who was "leaning on Jesus' bosom" (John 13:23) at the Last Supper. It had been at least fifty years since he had last seen the resurrected Jesus, and the two had certainly covered a lot of ground together during the Lord's earthly ministry. They had traveled, eaten, and gone hungry, probably laughed, and gotten wet together when it rained. They were old friends who had known and loved each other, and John had even looked after the Lord's mother after the crucifixion (John 19:27).

No Fear

As he began to receive the revelation, John turned around at the voice as of a trumpet, and as the sound of many waters. He saw the glorified Jesus Christ, and "fell at his feet as dead" (Rev. 1:17). It's a good thing old John had a strong heart because it must have skipped a few beats right then. The Scriptures tell us that Jesus "laid his right hand upon me, saying unto me, Fear not" (Rev. 1:17). Isn't that what we would expect from Jesus? John was probably scared out of his britches, and Jesus reached out His hand and put it on His old friend's shoulder to offer comfort and support.

Imagine if Jesus Christ were to appear to you in a moment of fear and anxiety, place His hand on your shoulder, and say, "Don't worry: I've got everything under control." If you believe the Bible is the Word of God, He already has. "Fear not, little flock; for it is your Father's good pleasure to give you the kingdom" (Luke 12:32). In Luke 12, Jesus tells us not to worry about our possessions or what we're going to eat, drink, or wear. We are not to have a doubtful mind or fret that things over which we have no control may turn against us. "But rather seek ye the kingdom of God; and all these things shall be added unto you" (v. 31).

Have you ever known a parent whose young child seemed constantly in torment and fear? You might have wondered what was wrong with the child, when suddenly it occurred to you the problem must be with the parent, not the child. What loving parent could possibly allow their child to be in a constant state of fear? In fact, the opposite is true. Parents want their children to know the warmth and comfort of love and to feel secure and protected. No parent loves their child any more than God loves His children.

"Be not afraid of sudden fear, neither of the desolation of the wicked, when it cometh" (Prov. 3:25). It must be terrible for a child not to have trust and confidence in his parents, and to be constantly fearful. Christians certainly should not feel that way toward God. He has never given us any reason not to have the utmost trust and confidence in Him so we aren't fearful. If we have a spirit of fear it's a signal to God that we don't believe in His ability and His commitment to deliver to us what He has promised. "But without faith it is impossible to please him: for he that cometh to God must believe that he is, and that he is a rewarder of them that diligently seek him" (Heb. 11: 6). A simple definition of faith is having the utmost trust and confidence that God is who He says He is, and believing that as a loving parent, He wants only the best for us.

Christians love, praise, and reverence a God who is merciful, holy, and righteous. In a book whose purpose is to dispel fear, it might seem contradictory at first glance to suggest the fears of the world are overcome through the fear of God. It is not, however, when we consider that the fear of God is usually defined absent the consideration of His attributes. We tend to define the fear of God from our perspective without consideration of what it means from God's perspective. The fear of God is a characteristic of born-again believers, but it also refers to a possessive quality of God. The Christian's fear of God translates into worship, reverence, and admiration that encourages our desire for fellowship with Him and exhorts us to righteousness. But in order to fully appreciate the fear of God we must also understand it in the context of who He is and as one of His personal attributes. We will discuss the fear of God in a reciprocal context as the partnership between the believer and the Lord, and as a key element in living a joyous life free from fear.

Exodus 20:5-6 says God will visit "the iniquity of the fathers upon the children unto the third and fourth generation of them that hate me; And shewing mercy unto thousands of them that love me, and keep my commandments." According to the Jewish Talmud, this passage teaches that God's mercy and grace exceed His requirement for justice and punishment by at least five-hundred-fold. The word *thousands* is plural, implying at least two thousand generations. If we take this literally and do the math, we find that God's mercy considerably outweighs His attribute for justice by well over a factor of 500. The fear of a just, holy, and righteous God cannot be understood if it's considered separate from His great mercy. Because the fear of the Lord is a partnership between the believer and God, the believer has specific responsibilities to fulfill in order to enjoy the full fruit of His mercy and grace.

A brief explanation of this book's title is in order. Whether we have faith in Christ or not, all of us have mountains to overcome and dragons to slay. Mountains are large, immovable objects that often stand between us and the objectives we wish to achieve or the things we want from life. We can either subdue mountains or we can walk around them. If we decide to walk around them we probably won't get where we want to go when we want to get there, if we get there at all. We can also succumb to fear and walk away from mountains. They aren't likely to follow us, but we will fall short of God's purpose for our lives if we do so.

Dragons are a different matter. Of course, the head dragon master is Satan. Dragons use our fears against us to prevent us from overcoming mountains. They must either be subdued or served. If we try to walk around them or away from them they chase us until we either turn around and fight, or surrender. They never go away. Dragons may sometimes take the guise of another person, but more frequently, they camouflage themselves inside that person we see in the mirror every morning. Wherever we find them, the one thing they all have in common is that they exploit our fears. We can't do anything to change Satan, and we can't do a whole lot more to change anyone else. But through Jesus Christ, we can have complete dominance over the dragons in our lives. Through Christ, we can hold the world by the tail in one hand and the dragon by the ear in the other. With His strength, we might even put the dragon to work serving the Lord's purpose.

The advantage that Christians with faith in Jesus have is that through Christ all mountains may be overcome and all dragons slain. The same can't be said for those without faith in Christ, because they have only their own limited strength to rely on. If we compare it to baseball, we may not always bat 1.000, but we will hit much higher with Christ than without Him, and we'll never strike out to end the game.

God is so merciful and gracious that He even wants to "deliver them who through fear of death were all their lifetime subject to bondage" (Heb. 2:15). Through Jesus Christ, we have been promised a new resurrected body and eternal life. It is His purpose that we not be held hostage by the normal fears of the world, death, or the prospect of eternal torment. He offers us a life free from fear, and it is ours to either accept or reject.

Those who are consumed by matters of the flesh are subject to the fears that come with each new sunrise and the dread that rides on every wind of change. Christians with faith in Jesus, however, can boldly stand tall in a frequently troubled and shell-shocked world, in full trust and confidence that God is who He says He is, and that fear is not part of His agenda for our lives.

CHAPTER 1

HEADS OR TAILS?

There hath no temptation taken you but such
as is common to man.

—1 CORINTHIANS 10:13

THIS MAY BE a risky way to start a book, which has as its objective the overcoming of fear. In order to ensure no false expectations are created, it seems best to lay this matter on the table at the beginning. Every human being who has ever walked the earth, including Jesus Christ, has known fear. Further, none of us will ever reach an advanced state of spiritual enlightenment that will preclude us from experiencing fear in the future. Looking at our world, it seems there is an endless list of things over which we should fear and fret. The reason for this is that, as we will see shortly, the list really is endless. That's the bad news.

The good news is that through Jesus Christ, "The LORD

shall make thee the head, and not the tail; and thou shalt be above only, and thou shalt not be beneath" (Deut. 28:13). As the head and not the tail, we can have mastery over our fears so they serve God's purpose and ours. When our fears are resolved, they can serve as a source of strength and determination, not weakness. Confronting fear with the intent of reaching a full and final resolution will allow us to overcome the mountains that tower in each of our lives with strong confidence. That doesn't necessarily mean you'll be ready for your first set of skydiving lessons by the time you finish this book, but losing the fear of flying may be within reach.

Captain Humble

In 2 Kings 1, the king of Samaria was on his deathbed and wanted to speak with the prophet Elijah. It is fair to assume the king did not have Elijah's best interest in mind. Ahaziah was a wicked king without the fear of God, and he sent a captain with fifty of his men to the top of a hill where Elijah was, with the intent of hauling him back to Samaria. In verse 10, the captain ordered Elijah down from the hill, saying:

> Thou man of God, the king hath said, Come down. And Elijah answered and said to the captain of fifty, If I be a man of God, then let fire come down from heaven, and consume thee and thy fifty. And there came down fire from heaven, and consumed him and his fifty.

The king sent another captain with his fifty and the same thing happened to them. Apparently Ahaziah didn't waver from his purpose of seeing Elijah, even after two captains and one hundred men were consumed by fire from heaven. We are not told the name of the third captain the king sent, but we can safely surmise he was a man who feared God. The third captain of fifty fell on his knees before Elijah and pleaded, "O man of God, I pray thee, let my life, and the life of these fifty thy servants, be precious in thy sight" (2 Kings 1:13). The angel of the Lord spared the captain and his men, and Elijah went with him to Ahaziah in Samaria and passed a death sentence on the king. This is an example of fear that is good, because it saved the precious life of the captain and his fifty men.

MISPLACING THE FEAR OF GOD

Abraham was a "friend of God" (James 2:23), yet not all of the examples he left are as favorable as the example made by the third captain of fifty. In fact, Abraham left us with one very unseemly example of what unfounded fear can do to a great man of faith. In Genesis 20:2, "Abraham said of Sarah his wife, She is my sister: and Abimelech king of Gerar sent, and took Sarah." She was probably going to be one of the king's concubines, but after the king found out he had taken another man's wife, he confronted Abraham. Abraham made an excuse for himself and said, "I thought, Surely the fear of God is not in this place; and they will slay me for my wife's sake" (v. 11). He was so worried about saving his own skin he would have allowed his wife to be compromised by another man.

Abimelech gave Sarah back to Abraham, and told her, "Behold, he is to thee a covering of the eyes, unto all that are with thee, and with all other: thus she was reproved" (v. 16). Most of us can probably remember when we have done something so embarrassing that we wanted to cover our eyes with our hands in shame. The embarrassment is no less acute when someone we love is motivated by fear and does something shameful. Abraham didn't think anyone in Gerar had the fear of God, and he must have misplaced his or left it outside the town gate or he wouldn't have placed

Sarah in such a compromising position. Because he failed to have trust and confidence in God's ability to deliver on all His promises, Abraham's fear caused him to behave shamefully. It's just as true today that when we fail to have trust and confidence in God, our fears will come upon us and we will bring shame to ourselves and our loved ones.

Fear, Failure, and Faith

The only similarity between the stories of the third captain of fifty and Abraham is that they both faced fear. The captain knew the previous two captains and their companies were consumed by fire from heaven; he was in no hurry to join them. Nevertheless, he was probably afraid of disobeying King Ahaziah's command, so he followed orders and went to the hill where Elijah was. He was caught between a rock and a hard place, so he humbled himself before God and asked for mercy.

Abraham, on the other hand, was a prosperous herdsman who probably didn't have to settle in Gerar in the first place. The incident with Abimelech occurred before Isaac was born, so it seems Abraham used his failure in this case to strengthen his resolve in the fear of God. Failure is as certain as sunrise, and as long as it strengthens our relationship with the Lord it isn't something to be feared. Abraham's failure in Gerar was part of the strong foundation of faith that gave him the trust in God to offer his only son, Isaac, in sacrifice (Gen. 22:10).

"There hath no temptation taken you but such as is common to man: but God is faithful, who will not suffer you to be tempted above that ye are able; but will with the temptation also make a way to escape, that ye may be able to bear it" (1 Cor. 10:13). Temptation takes many forms, to include fear and uncertainty, but we need not allow it to overwhelm

4

us because God will always leave us a route of escape. If we do find ourselves in a hopeless situation the first step in resolving it is to recognize we created it, not God. God can get us out of the hopeless situations we get ourselves into, but He likely will not do it until we acknowledge our responsibility in creating the mess we are in.

Before we get too deeply involved in discussion of the different types of fear and how they may be overcome, let's first examine where fear most frequently enters our lives. Fear is insidious and works incessantly to drain our faith in Christ and the joy from our lives. Fear is like a little drip of water underneath a road or building built on a loose foundation of sand. Drop by drop, tiny particles of sand are channeled away until a huge sinkhole develops underneath the foundation and the entire structure collapses. If we want to save the foundation of our faith, one of the best ways is to stop the dripping that undermines it. In the next chapter, we begin by identifying some of the most common and preventable causes of the fear that insinuates itself into our lives.

CHAPTER 2

TURNING DOWN THE VOLUME

> For God hath not given us the spirit of fear;
> but of power, and of love, and of a sound
> mind.
>
> —2 TIMOTHY 1:7

T HE SPIRIT OF fear is the antithesis of the spirit of the
fear of the Lord. In the United States and throughout
the world, many of our institutions are preoccupied
with imparting to each of us a spirit of fear. Intentionally
or otherwise, the spirit of fear has been mass-marketed in
a way that should make automobile manufactures envious.
The institutions that are intended to serve us instead gener-
ate fear as their primary product. This is a highly predictable outcome for one simple reason: where the fear of God
is not present, the spirit of fear is. That giant sucking sound
we hear is the spirit of fear filling the vacuum after the fear
of God is displaced.

This isn't a paranoid suggestion that a conspiracy exists

to instill a spirit of fear in the citizenry of the world so that one group or another may dominate us. If there is a conspiracy, then Satan is at the helm, not the Council of Foreign Relations or the Bilderberg Group. It's simply logical that a natural outgrowth of a turn away from the fear of God is a turn toward the spirit of fear. This seems to be a self-evident truth that should be easy to demonstrate.

Speaking in general terms, the two largest institutions most responsible for perpetuating the spirit of fear are governments and broadcast media. Both institutions overlap in places. For example, the media broadcasts information on politics and areas of public concern. The legislative, executive, and judicial sub-groups of our government are like the disk operating system on our computer: we don't always see it but it's behind the scenes, making sure everything runs smoothly. Like our disk operating system, sometimes it crashes. The broadcast media includes subgroups such as television, radio, Internet, newspapers, and entertainment. The media filters information from both government and private groups to the general public to entertain, inform, and influence.

These institutions focus relentlessly on issues that, in their opinion, we should be interested in and concerned about. What we must recognize is they also have an unhealthy fixation on issues intended to instill unnatural fears in the general public. In order to make this point, some of these issues of concern are provided in the list that follows. Your indulgence is asked, recognizing the list is not complete and is somewhat tedious. But please take a few moments to scan it. It contains items that, we are led to believe, could at any moment come crashing down around us with catastrophic results. Our lives would forever be changed for the worse, and we might even be killed along with those we love. In no order of merit these imminent crises-in-waiting are:

Terrorist attack
Global warming
Inflation
Crime
Computer viruses
Poverty
Famine
Nuclear proliferation
Anthrax
Sport utility vehicles
Earthquakes
Mad cow disease
Corporate mergers
Unhealthy fast food
Genetically engineered food
Malpractice by doctors
Taxes too high
Caffeine
Ground water pollution
Obesity
Drive-by shootings
Noise pollution
Social Security bankruptcy
Endangered species
Sexual predators
Sewage runoff
Illegal immigration
Diabetes
Political scandal
Corporate profits too high
Hollywood scandal
Balding
Urban sprawl
Flooding
Pestilence
Child pornography
Loss of manufacturing jobs

Poisoned water supply
Racism
Unemployment
Drug and alcohol abuse
Air pollution
Homelessness
Depleted ozone layer
Population explosion
Small pox
Decaying roads, bridges
Wildfires
Road rage
Toddlers drowning in
   buckets
Secondhand smoke
Gun control
Taxes too low
Pit bulls and other mean
   dogs
Skin cancer
Congestive heart failure
Home invasions
Loss of sex drive
Endangered rain forests
Aging population
Medicare bankruptcy
Rising credit card debt
Prostate cancer
Not enough exercise
Minimum wage too low
Rising home prices
Foreign imports
Recession
Hurricanes
HIV/AIDS
Gang violence
Dolphin meat in tuna fish

Drought	Public education crisis
Not enough prison cells	Too many prisons
West Nile virus	Decaying electrical power
Carpal tunnel syndrome	grid
Brain aneurysm	Human cloning
Too much salt in Chinese food	Attention deficit disorder
Wrinkles and brown spots	Traffic congestion
Pedophile clergy	Stroke

If, after scanning this list, someone disagrees that many of our public and private institutions are pushing a spirit of fear, there is nothing more I can say that will change their mind. In fact, there may be some who believe all these items are legitimate causes for concern and that it's the responsibility of every right-thinking person to stay informed and involved in providing solutions to all these problems. Well, perhaps they are right. One thing you won't find on this list, however, is Jesus Christ.

TIME OUT

Granted, almost all of these issues are serious. Certainly if your child was one of the handful around the world who has drowned in a bucket, that would be a very serious issue for you. But the majority of these issues are either beyond our control, manufactured, inflated, or irrelevant to our day-to-day living. They are presented as a pending crisis, or something we should be interested in, by non-Christians who do not hold a biblical worldview. We should be wary of placing importance on someone else's agenda for our focus of interest, particularly when Jesus Christ is deliberately excluded from every aspect of it.

When we listen to our government leaders and media outlets, we must recognize most of them do not fear God. Therefore, they most likely have an unhealthy spirit of fear, which they broadcast toward us. Believers overcome the spirit of fear through their faith in Jesus Christ. "For this is the love of God, that we keep his commandments: and his commandments are not grievous. For whatsoever is born of God overcometh the world: and this is the victory that overcometh the world, even our faith" (1 John 5:3–4).

What does "overcometh the world" mean? That laundry list of potential crises is one place to start overcoming the world. This is the same endless list of bad things that can happen that was mentioned at the beginning of Chapter 1, containing all the things we can be fearful of and fret over. You could draw up your own list and add to it, but don't waste your time. Christians don't need to be worried about all those things. Remember Jesus' words in Luke 12:32: "Fear not, little flock." He has them under control.

Christians should stay informed about what is happening in the world, and if called to help address some of these problems we should do so. If some of these issues affect your life, you have my sympathy and prayer. But as a general rule, Christians should sweep away the concerns of the world like a street cleaner sweeping the filth out of a roadside gutter.

In 1 John 4:1, the apostle tells us, "Believe not every spirit, but try the spirits whether they are of God." Verse 4 says, "Ye are of God, little children, and have overcome them: because greater is he that is in you, than he that is in the world." The spirit of fear is not of God and we should not listen to it. In practical terms this means we shouldn't be worrying or losing sleep over things like Social Security bankruptcy, increased solar flare activity, or getting nuked by radioactive dirty bombs.

This doesn't mean Christians are fatalistic. We're not like King Ahab in 1 Kings 22, who marched with his eyes wide open into disaster. He was out of the will of God because he and his wife, Jezebel, were extremely wicked. Had Ahab listened to God's warning through the prophet Micaiah he wouldn't have gone to Ramoth-gilead to do battle. He went anyway, and a certain man fired off an arrow at nothing in particular (v. 34). God must have retrofitted that arrow in mid-flight with a laser-guided seeker-head because it crossed Ahab's T right at the shoulder blades. Ahab's number was up, and there was no chance he would leave Ramoth-gilead alive after he ignored God's warning.

The key for Christians is to have a healthy fear of God and stay within His will. If we are within His will, there shouldn't be any reason to fear stray arrows. We should be "confident of this very thing, that he which hath begun a good work in you will perform it until the day of Jesus Christ" (Phil. 1:6). God won't call us home until we accomplish what He has set out for us. We don't need to worry about the devil thwarting God's plans for our lives because they are dictated by the Lord's timetable, not Satan's. If we go off course like Ahab there may be cause for concern, but God certainly doesn't expect us to worry about silly things that only drain the joy out of our lives.

WHAT, ME WORRY?

Something that has certainly increased in the last one hundred years is the amount of noise we are exposed to. With the amount of print, electronic, and visual media we are exposed to one would think the eyes and ears of a born-again Christian are trash cans for unbelievers to pour their garbage into. In Los Angeles for example, drivers are subjected daily to a billboard assault that is truly amazing, and other major cities in the U. S. are no different. Scantily clad women that work at "gentlemen's clubs" practically splash off the billboards through the car windshield and into your lap. The 24-hour, 7-day per week news cycle operates under the false premise there is more than 3 minutes of daily news worth listening to when there isn't. Just because one hundred politicians stand in front of one hundred microphones, it's presumed they have at least one meaningful word to say. They usually don't. Christians should have better things to do with their time than waste it on political wrangling, the latest exotic disease or murder trial de jour, or whatever else a godless society thinks is important. If we are spending too much time on these things we are not overcoming the world like we should. We should learn "to number our days, that we may apply our hearts unto wisdom" (Ps. 90:12) instead of being entwined in meaningless pursuits that only feed our baser instincts and the spirit of fear.

It is not being suggested here that Christians should tune out the world, but turning down the volume might be a good idea. There is a tremendous amount of noise that is passed off as "news" and "entertainment," which is really nothing more than godless chatter. Before anyone complains, no attempt is being made here to sound prudish. "All things are lawful unto me, but all things are not expedient: all things are lawful for me, but I will not be brought under the power of any" (1 Cor. 6:12). If someone wants to watch Jerry Springer or listen ad nauseam to the latest Hollywood murder/rape/divorce/shoplifting/drug trial, that's their business. But if Christians constantly fill their minds with the work product of an unbeliever's imagination, it should come as no surprise when we find ourselves receiving something of their spirit.

If your bathroom faucet was slowly dripping and driving you nuts when you're trying to sleep, you would either turn it off or get it fixed right away. Our government and media are dripping fear into us like an executioner intravenously injecting lethal poison into a death row inmate strapped on a gurney. It is within our power to turn off the fear, or at least lower the volume to an easily manageable and tolerable level. The only information addiction Christians should have is for Christ and the Bible. That is the first step in confronting and overcoming the mountains and dragons in our lives.

CHAPTER 3

LOVE MEANS TAKING A BULLET FOR THE OTHER GUY

> Beloved, let us love one another: for love is of God; and everyone that loveth is born of God, and knoweth God.
>
> —1 JOHN 4:7

I F WE SPEND our idle time listening to and watching the endless babbling of unbelievers on the radio, television, etc., we needlessly expose ourselves to their spirit of fear, specifically the fear of death. Jesus delivers "them who through fear of death were all their lifetime subject to bondage" (Heb. 2:15). People that are in bondage are slaves. People who don't believe in Jesus are in slavery to their fear of death. We know this is true because the Bible says so, and we know it from personal experience.

Death is a subject that will come up throughout our discussion because it lies at the root of most, if not all of our fears. Fear often results from uncertainty, and although there is nothing uncertain about the fact that we will die, the manner and timing of it are unknown. It is also fair to say there is uncertainty about what happens afterwards, although those with faith in Christ have a better idea of what to expect than those without. The fact that there may also be pain associated with dying causes us to look forward to it without enthusiasm.

Strangely, the world has a morbid preoccupation with death that the Christian should not share. If you take a quick look at the list in the last chapter of the bad things that can happen to us, you may notice at least twenty different ways to die are mentioned and more could be added. There are probably hundreds, maybe even thousands of ways to die, and if a new way were invented, that would be front-page news. There are thousands of bad things that can happen to us every day: ranging from hangnails to fender benders, to broken bones, or sudden death. We can worry about all those things, or listen to Jesus who says, "Fear not, little flock" (Luke 12:32).

When we are filled with a spirit of fear and in bondage to the fear of death, we aren't filled with the love of God. First John 4:18 says, "There is no fear in love; but perfect love casteth out fear: because fear hath torment. He that feareth is not made perfect in love." Let's hold 1 John 4:18 in front of a mirror and see what it says. "There is no love in fear; but fear casts out perfect love: because love hath no torment. He that is perfect in love has no fear." Before we understand how this works, we must first be clear on what it means to love someone.

Overcoming Supernatural Fear

Greater love hath no man than this, that a man lay down his life for his friends.

—John 15:13

Judah stood before the prime minister of Egypt (not knowing the prime minister was his brother Joseph), ready to lay down his life for his youngest brother, Benjamin (Gen. 44:33). Jesus did lay down His life for all of us. That type of love isn't an excessively sentimental, heart-wrenching, misty-eyed outpouring of emotion. It isn't necessarily romantic, and it most definitely isn't sex. It's like a scene from a war movie where a soldier covers a hand grenade with his body, or takes a bullet meant for someone else. These examples fit the biblical definition of love.

When someone loves another, they are placing the same value on that other person's soul and spirit as they place on their own. Loving a person means valuing them as much as God does. Jesus Christ is the only person who has ever been perfect in love. Only Jesus' shed blood was of sufficient value to redeem all mankind. Jesus placed the same value on our souls as He placed on His own, and He paid the terrible price we could never afford.

The ecumenical council at Chalcedon in 451 A.D. reaffirmed the full and complete humanity of Jesus Christ, both before and after His resurrection. This was a response to heretics who claimed that Jesus, as God, could not experience suffering and therefore was not fully a man. Not that it's important what I think, but I see Scripture the same way those folks at Chalcedon saw it. Jesus Christ is fully man and fully God, and if anyone wants to argue that point, they may feel free to do so elsewhere.

Somewhere is told the story of a man driving home with his little boy, when an angry wasp got in the car and was looking for someone to sting. The man didn't want his little boy stung so he reached out and squashed the wasp with his hand. He got stung in the process, and when they got home about fifteen minutes later, his hand was

17

swelling up a bit and it hurt. His wife took out a sharp needle and tweezers, dug the stinger out and poured iodine inside the little hole in his hand. She smiled at him and said, "Now that didn't hurt a bit, did it?" He grimaced and said, "Compared to having it cauterized by a red-hot ingot from a blacksmith's furnace, it didn't hurt at all." When Jesus died for us on the cross the pain He endured was infinitely greater than a wasp sting or deep burn. Anybody who minimizes His agony is heaping scorn on the Son of God and trying to diminish the greatness of His sacrifice. When Jesus Christ was on that cross His pain and suffering was greater than anything we can imagine, and anyone who says otherwise is blaspheming His name and work.

All the Gospels, with the exception of John, describe Jesus' anguish prior to His arrest and crucifixion. It is important for us to remember the grace and courage of Jesus as He went to the cross. Grace is when someone does something for a person that he doesn't have to, with no expectation of ever being paid back. We have no way to pay back either Jesus the man or Jesus as God. His grace, strength, and courage as He went to the cross for us were remarkable. It was clearly something He wasn't looking forward to, and in fact it is fair to say He was fearful. In Mark 14:36 Jesus says, "Abba, Father, all things are possible unto thee; take away this cup from me: nevertheless not what I will, but what thou wilt." Jesus Christ the man feared the excruciating agony of crucifixion, made infinitely worse by the bearing of our sins on His sinless perfection. The fact that He also happened to be God didn't make it any easier to endure the agony. In fact, it made it worse to a degree we can't even begin to appreciate.

Jesus had to overcome His personal fear as a man in order to redeem us. He was able to overcome His fear because He placed His full trust and confidence in God. In Mark 14:36, Jesus essentially stated His preference to God the Father that He would rather not go through with the crucifixion. But in the same breath He placed His fate completely in the hands of the Father with absolute conviction and determination. As the fully human Son of God, the fear He overcame is identical to the fear you or I would have experienced in that situation, but magnified to an extent we will never be able to grasp. The fact that He had to overcome fear of supernatural proportions makes the actions of Jesus the man greater than any words of worship, praise, or gratitude can proclaim. He was only able to overcome that fear because of His perfect love for us.

The perfect love of Jesus Christ drives out the spirit of fear in born-again Christians. He provides us an example of perfect love, and the price He paid in doing so is far greater than anything we can comprehend. It doesn't matter how long we live, or how hard or frightening life may be at times, or how much pain we suffer, we can never reach the level of suffering He endured for our sakes. It may seem our capacity to fear is unlimited while our capacity to love is finite, but that isn't the case with Jesus. He has love without measure, and has given it to us to drive away our spirit of fear with confidence and with power. Love doesn't always come without a price. Jesus makes His love available to us if we need strength to make the kind of sacrifices that love often requires. With that strength also comes the courage to break free from bondage to fear, and to unhesitatingly make sacrifices with determination.

CHAPTER 4

DEFINING THE FEAR OF GOD AS...HMMM

And there shall come forth a rod out of the stem of Jesse, and a Branch shall grow out of his roots: And the spirit of the LORD shall rest upon him, the spirit of wisdom and understanding, the spirit of counsel and might, the spirit of knowledge and of the fear of the LORD; And shall make him of quick understanding in the fear of the LORD.

—ISAIAH 11:1–3

ANY LOVING PARENT would teach their small child to fear strange men soliciting them from a passing car, or a big mean dog running at them with drool foaming out of his mouth. We want our children to fear these things for their own good. God also wants us to fear Him not for His sake, but for our own good. He defines precisely what He means by this type of fear, and it is different from that of a child meeting a pedophile or a mean dog, but it preserves us just the same.

When we fail to understand the fear of God in accordance with His definition and in context with who He is, we fall short in appreciating how wonderful God is. Isaiah 11:1–3, a prophecy of the coming Messiah, teaches us

21

that even Jesus knew the fear of the Lord. The fear of God should be a positive feature of every Christian's character. We should share the same goals and aspirations for our life that God has for us so we have a common interest. The fear of God gives us a standard to follow so we don't stray too far off course as we accomplish the Lord's plan for our life. It serves as an anchor we can rely on to prevent us from drifting away from foundational truth.

Many verses in the Bible define the fear of God. Although not all-inclusive, the following verses provide good definitions:

- ❖ Proverbs 1:7; 8:13; 9:10; 14:16; 19:23
- ❖ Job 28:28
- ❖ Deuteronomy 6:24
- ❖ Psalms 34:9; 111:10

A consolidated summary and paraphrase of these verses is offered for convenience:

> The fear of the LORD is to hate evil. It is the beginning of wisdom and knowledge. Knowledge of the holy God gives us good understanding, that we do His commandments and depart from evil. Fear the LORD for our good always that He may preserve us alive, give us strong confidence and a place of refuge, that we will be satisfied and without want, and not visited with evil.

Perhaps some of you parents can relate to the following analogy. You tell your child not to play with matches so they don't burn themselves. The child ignores your warning and plays with matches anyway, gets burned, and then gets mad at you because you were right. If the child had feared the parent in the same context that we fear

God, the child's love, reverence, and respect for the wisdom of the parent would have precluded his playing with matches. He got burned because of his disobedience, and the consequences he paid were not because of anything the parent did. The same holds true in our relationship with God. We can be disobedient if we choose, but the consequences we have to face are not because of anything God has done wrong.

THE FEAR OF THE LORD— A CHARACTERISTIC OF GOD

Parents tell their child not to play with matches because they love their child, and are fearful the child will be harmed by being burned. This is fear from the perspective of the parent. The fact is, many parents are so fearful for the well-being of their child they would lay down their life to protect them from harm. The fear of God may also be understood in the same context. God is fearful that if we are disobedient and engage in all sorts of sinful behavior, harm will come upon us. Because He loves us He wants to keep us from harm, so He warns us. In simplest terms, He worries about us.

Part of understanding the fear of God comes with the recognition that God is sovereign. He created the universe and He makes the rules, such as the one that says fire is hot and will burn us if handled improperly. Apparently Satan had a problem with the fact that God is sovereign, and the famous five "I will's" of Isaiah 14 give us a good idea of why he's in hot water with the Lord.

> How art thou fallen from heaven, O Lucifer, [or O day
>   star] son of the morning! how art thou cut down
>   to the ground, which didst weaken the nations! For
>   thou hast said in thine heart,
> I will ascend into heaven,

I will exalt my throne above the stars of God:
I will sit also upon the mount of the congregation, in
   the sides of the north:
I will ascend above the heights of the clouds;
I will be like the most High.

—Isaiah 14:12–14

Like a little child, Satan wanted to play with matches and he got mad at God when he got burned. He didn't think getting burned was fair, so he tried to snatch God's sovereign right to declare fire as hot out of His hands. No parent is going to surrender their sovereign right to make decisions to a child, because the child lacks the discernment to judge wisely. Neither is the Creator going to surrender His sovereignty to Satan or anyone else, because all created beings fall short of His glory. When we fear God, we recognize and agree with Him that the only One qualified and up to the task of being God is God.

Understanding the fear of God from God's perspective also helps us understand why and how Jesus was able to bear the unimaginable anguish He suffered on the cross. He could have called forth "more than twelve legions of angels" (Matt. 26:53) at any time to avoid His agony, but the fear of God prevented Him. Jesus knew that without His death on the cross mankind would be left adrift without a savior or redeemer, doomed to eternal destruction. His love and God's fearfulness for what would happen to mankind without His sacrifice gave Jesus the man the strength He needed to complete His excruciating purpose.

The Fear of the Lord—
A Characteristic of Man

The fear of God is discussed throughout the Bible, and is mentioned at least twenty times in the Book of Proverbs alone. The central theme that binds all these verses together and defines the specific action man must accomplish to fear God is this: God expects us to hate evil.

We will be on the receiving end of many of God's gracious gifts if we fear Him. Wisdom, understanding, strong confidence, refuge from evil, peace, security, safety, and satisfaction are all promised to us at no cost if we fear God. These aren't things we take from someone else because of our great strength, courage, and personal integrity. We don't earn wisdom because of our keen intellect, and we don't have a refuge from evil because of our good behavior and self-righteousness. We don't have inner peace because we have cleverly invented it, and we don't have strong confidence and freedom from fear because we can outsmart anything the world throws our way. These are gifts of grace from God.

We can't do any of these things by our own strength, but it is within our capacity to hate evil. "Hating evil" has a different verbal texture than "fearing God." Understanding the full meaning of the term "fear of God" requires an inclusive definition from both God's perspective and ours. When defined solely from the perspective of the individual Christian, the fear of God can be understood simply as a hatred of evil. If we hate evil, we have also fulfilled God's expectation of us that we fear Him.

The fear of God carries a negative implication for many people who understand it out of context. It is wrongly associated with intolerant religious extremists who want to impose their beliefs on others, based on a God whose existence is tenuous at best. Most people, on the other hand, would agree that hating evil is prudent and wise. Of course, there are still others who would deny the existence of evil at all and believe that morality is relative. But for now the existence of evil, and sovereign God-given truth as the foundation of joyful living and freedom from fear, will be deferred for later discussion.

The Fruits of the Fear of God

"The fruit of the Spirit is love, joy, peace, longsuffering, gentleness, goodness, faith, meekness, temperance: against such there is no law" (Gal. 5:22–23). The fear of God also brings with it the fruits of strong confidence, wisdom and knowledge, satisfaction, and love that are capable of casting out any of the fears that may confront us. "The secret of the LORD is with them that fear him; and he will shew them his covenant" (Ps. 25:14). God has a tendency to hide many of His secret things out in broad daylight. We have become so sophisticated we can't see them anymore. The fruits of the fear of God aren't hidden from anyone but are within reach of all those who seek after Him.

The fear of God is not one single thing and it doesn't fit an easy definition. It encompasses the partnership between the believer and the triune God, and it must be understood from the perspective of both partners in the relationship. It is something believers must embrace each and every day in their walk with the Lord, because it is never going to be finished or reach an end. Our fear of God is tested on a daily basis, providing numerous opportunities to embrace evil or react with ambivalence toward it.

The Lord's Prayer in Matthew 6:11–13 says, "Give us this day our daily bread... And lead us not into temptation, but deliver us from evil." Our resolve will be tested daily, and daily we will be given the chance to do evil. It is the fear of God, through the strength of Christ and the Holy Spirit, that delivers us from evil many times throughout the course of each day. If we pass through a single day without awareness of Christ's role in delivering us from committing an evil act, or safeguarding us against someone else's evil action, then we aren't paying attention.

We are constantly under assault from the fears and temptations of the world, and we must recognize them so that through Christ they can be deflected away and not allowed to plant roots. We must also have full trust and confidence that God fears for our well-being, and that as a loving parent wants to guard us from evil and harm. If we keep our end of the bargain—that is the fear of the Lord—we can be absolutely certain God will keep His end as well.

CHAPTER 5

THE SCHOOL OF HARD KNOCKS: EXAMPLE OF THE PATRIARCHS

Let us hear the conclusion of the whole matter:
Fear God, and keep his commandments: for
this is the whole duty of man.
—ECCLESIASTES 12:13

THERE IS NOT a more concise declaration of what sovereign God expects from His creation than these words of King Solomon, written almost three thousand years ago. "Solomon's wisdom excelled the wisdom of all the children of the east country, and all the wisdom of Egypt. For he was wiser than all men; than Ethan the Ezrahite, and Heman, and Chalcol, and Darda, the sons of Mahol: and his fame was in all nations round about" (1 Kings 4:30–31). Scripture doesn't say anything more about Ethan or any of the sons of Mahol, but thankfully it does say quite a bit about Solomon.

King Solomon fell short of the mark when it came to fearing God and keeping His commandments. He multiplied

29

wives and horses, spent too much time building his palace, and "did evil in the sight of the LORD" (1 Kings 11:6). Solomon allowed his wives to turn his heart away "from the LORD God of Israel, which had appeared unto him twice" (1 Kings 11:9). As a result, his kingdom was subsequently divided under his son, Rehoboam, never to return to its former glory. The grim reality that a man with Solomon's great wisdom should fail so spectacularly is a sobering reminder that self-indulgence and pride are common maladies even to the wisest among us. Solomon embraced evil when he embraced his many wives, tarnishing what should have been a glorious legacy. He feared for the happiness of his wives, and forgot the fear of the Lord. Yet, God's love for Solomon never wavered, and it was presumably late in life that he was brought back into the fold.

THE GENESIS OF FEAR

The first time we meet with fear in the Bible is Genesis 3:10. Adam heard God walking about in the Garden of Eden when he realized he and Eve weren't wearing a stitch of clothing, and he was afraid. God hadn't done anything to make Adam afraid of Him. In fact, God had been quite generous with Adam, giving him a nice garden to live in with plenty of food and good company. Adam had dominion over all the fish, all the fowl, all the beasts, and the entire earth. God had even given him the breath of life, creating Adam in His own image, a thing God didn't have to do. God hadn't done anything mean or harsh to Adam, so why was he afraid?

We all know the story. Adam wasn't afraid of God because of anything God had done. Adam was afraid because he had committed an act of rebellion. The Lord had established one single boundary for Adam's protection that he wasn't to cross, and because God loved Adam and is sovereign He had a right to do that. Adam ignored that boundary, one that should have been easy to stay within and was not burdensome. The understanding that consequences are associated with disobedience probably came to Adam upon the realization he was naked. Whatever it was that kept him from realizing his nakedness before was gone, and Adam is the one who got rid of it. He was responsible for bringing fear upon himself.

"He that committeth sin is of the devil; for the devil sinneth from the beginning. For this purpose the Son of God was manifested, that he might destroy the works of the devil" (1 John 3:8). One of the works of the devil that Christ came to destroy was the unnatural fear brought down on mankind by the sin of Adam. It was not God's original purpose that Adam, or you and I for that matter, experience fear. There's no point in beating around the bush on this point: Adam made the mess, and Jesus is the one who's going to clean it up. That was true during the time of Adam and it's just as true today. There probably are not many parents who enjoy cleaning up after their spoiled brats and it probably isn't the Lord's favorite job, either. But He does it all the time and never complains because He loves us.

RIGHTEOUSNESS AND FILTHY RAGS

> And fear not them which kill the body, but are not able to kill the soul: but rather fear him which is able to destroy both soul and body in hell.
> —MATTHEW 10:28

This is something that needs to be addressed early. There are people who will use verses like Matthew 10:28 to say, "Aha, Aha! So God really is a big old meanie who's going to send good people I know and love to hell for eternal torment just because they don't believe in Jesus. That isn't fair!" This is partially true and will be discussed in more detail later.

For now, it is enough to note this statement is half-true when argued from a position of self-righteousness. Unbelievers will often claim to be as good and righteous as Christians are. This claim is probably true, but not a point worth debating. Isaiah 64:6 offers one of the less subtle and more vivid analogies God provides to deal with the self-righteous: "But we are all as an unclean thing, and all our righteousnesses are as filthy rags." Everyone has a pile of filthy rags somewhere in their home that they use for cleaning, maybe under the kitchen sink or out in the garage. We need look no further than the nearest trash can to remind ourselves what God thinks of our goodness and righteousness.

Matthew 10:28 should not be a source of confusion or present a dilemma for Christians. When we understand the fear of God in context with His great mercy, we understand that God's universal purpose is not eternal torment, but the promise of eternal life with Jesus Christ. "Having made known unto us the mystery of his will, according to his good pleasure which he hath purposed in himself: That in the dispensation of the fulness of times he might gather together in one all things in Christ, both which are in heaven, and which are on earth; even in him" (Eph 1:9–10). This is God's purpose, but not all the beings He created share that purpose, nor will He force anyone into compliance. If He had wanted to make everyone agree with Him, He would have created a race of space robots instead of mule-headed human beings.

EXAMPLES OF ABRAHAM, ISAAC, AND A FAMILY OF RASCALS

And he said, Lay not thine hand upon the lad, neither do thou any thing unto him: for now I know that thou fearest God, seeing thou hast not withheld thy son, thine only son from me.

—GENESIS 22:12

So spoke God on Mount Moriah after Abraham offered Isaac up for sacrifice. Hebrews 11:17–19 tells us Abraham reckoned God would raise up Isaac from the dead as a type of the resurrection of Jesus. He may not have known all the details of how that was supposed to happen, but because Abraham feared God and offered up his only son, God promised through "thy seed shall all the nations of the earth be blessed" (Gen. 22:18). "Abraham believed God, and it was imputed unto him for righteousness: and he was called the Friend of God" (James 2:23). To be a "friend of God" is as good as it gets.

Josephus[1] informs us that Isaac was about twenty-five years old when Abraham offered him to God, dispelling perceptions that he was merely an infant in arms. That would make Abraham about 125 years old, indicating Isaac was completely obedient to both God and his earthly father in this matter. Presumably, a young Isaac could have overpowered his aged father if he hadn't consented to the sacrifice. Isaac may have been more curious about the details of the resurrection than his father, but if so, the Bible is silent. His obedient submission is one of the outstanding examples of respect and fear of God in the Bible.

In Genesis 31, we find Isaac's son, Jacob, complaining about his father-in-law, Laban, who had been cheating him for the previous twenty years. In verse 42 Jacob says "Except the God of my father, the God of Abraham, and the fear of Isaac, had been with me," he (Jacob) would surely have been sent away empty-handed. In verse 53, of the same chapter, Jacob swore "by the fear of his father Isaac." This curious phrase, "fear of Isaac," is a clear reference to God but

33

receives no further explanation. The Bible tells us surprisingly little about Isaac, but we can surmise he had a unique relationship with God because of his obedient submission on Mount Moriah.

Isaac must have thought he was near death again when he told his oldest son, Esau, to "make me savoury meat, such as I love, and bring it to me, that I may eat; that my soul may bless thee before I die" (Gen. 27:4). Isaac's wife, Rebekah, was eavesdropping and helped Jacob fool Isaac to steal Esau's blessing for himself. When Esau found out, he was mad enough to kill Jacob. Rebekah told Jacob to get out of town and go to her brother Laban. She was so afraid for Jacob's life she probably packed some of that savoury meat into his lunch bucket while it was still hot and told him to buy a toothbrush when he got there. If Rebekah had shown more fear and trust in God she might have saved her boy Jacob a lot of trouble.

Now Jacob was on the run, and poor old Isaac, so near death, wouldn't see him until four wives, eleven sons, one daughter, and about twenty years later. Jacob was Isaac's youngest son, and he was a rascal, which he probably inherited from his mother's side of the family. On his way out of town Jacob stopped at a spot he would later call Bethel, where

> He took of the stones of that place, and put them for his pillows, and lay down in that place to sleep. And he dreamed, and behold a ladder set up on the earth, and the top of it reached to heaven: and behold the angels of God ascending and descending on it.
>
> —Genesis 28:11–12

Jesus referred to this incident in John 1:51, when he said, "Hereafter ye shall see heaven open, and the angels of God ascending and descending upon the Son of man."

Stone pillows make for cold comfort so Jacob probably didn't sleep well. He "awaked out of his sleep, and he said, Surely the Lord is in this place; and I knew it not. And he was afraid, and said, How dreadful [awesome] is this place! This is none other but the house of God, and this is the gate of heaven" (Gen. 28:16–17).

He was afraid, but judging from his later behavior, he was probably more afraid of his brother Esau than God at this point. Jacob had dreamed of the gate of heaven but he still had a few lessons to learn before God would change his name to Israel (Gen. 32:28). Jacob went to stay with his Uncle Laban, a man who could have used a lesson on the fear of God himself. Laban put Jacob to work and tested his mettle for the next twenty years as Jacob started a family. Jacob's children didn't turn out to be angels. It wasn't until many years later that he finally had his household "put away the strange gods" (Gen. 35:2) that his wife, Rachel, had stolen from her father, Laban. Despite his vision of a ladder to heaven with angels on it, Jacob wasn't a quick study when it came to learning the fear of God. He spent the better part of his life wrestling with his personal dragons, instead of slaying them early when he had a chance.

A person is never too old and it is never too late to learn the fear of God. Moses was forty when he left Egypt the first time, and like Jacob he tended flocks for his father-in-law. But in Moses' case it was for forty years. Moses had to ripen to the age of eighty before learning enough humility and fear of the Lord to be of any use to God.

One might think as a person got to be seventy or eighty years old, they would become more receptive to a testimony about Jesus Christ. After all, the older we get the more often we begin to hear the footsteps of the Grim

Reaper. By this time, most people have suffered quite a few hard knocks in life. So, time is going to either tenderize a person's heart or harden it. By the time they reach old age, either a person has learned to count their blessings and become more soft and gentle, or they have forgotten all the blessings and remember only the bitter struggles and hard times.

A friend of mine, a man of about eighty, spent most of his time taking care of his wife at home. He is not hard-hearted, but he would fall into the category of agnostic. His wife was confined to a wheelchair and was in a terribly desperate physical condition with all manner of maladies. I asked him where he got the strength to carry on every day. He said he got the strength to carry on from himself. His remaining objective in life was to make his wife as comfortable as possible until she dies, and that afterward he dies with a minimum of pain. That's mighty cold comfort, like using stones for pillows and dirt as a blanket.

Although Jacob may not have been a quick study in the fear of God we can surmise he learned it by the time he met Pharaoh in Egypt. "And Jacob said unto Pharaoh, The days of the years of my pilgrimage are an hundred and thirty years: few and evil have the days of the years of my life been, and have not attained unto the days of the years of the life of my fathers in the days of their pilgrimage" (Gen. 47:9). The Lord spent a good deal of time sweeping up after Jacob and his twelve boys, starting from about Genesis 28 through to the end of the book. Jacob knew that God had looked out for his family from beginning to end, and no matter how bad a mess he and his sons made the Lord was always one step ahead of them. If you have ever taken a dog for a walk with a leash and a choke chain then you probably know how Jesus feels after dealing with

Jacob, his twelve sons, and you and me. A dog will pull on a leash even though his eyes are popping out of his head if he wants to go somewhere, and sometimes people aren't any different.

"And when Jacob had made an end of commanding his sons, he gathered up his feet into the bed, and yielded up the ghost, and was gathered unto his people" (Gen. 49:33).

In verse 24 Jacob had blessed Joseph, whose "hands were made strong by the hands of the mighty God of Jacob." Jacob blessed his boys, gave funeral instructions, picked his feet up into bed, and committed his soul into the hands of the mighty God with trust and confidence.

That eighty-year-old friend of mine I mentioned doesn't want to lean on God because he says he doesn't want to be a hypocrite. He doesn't have the spirit of the fear of God, but although he won't admit it he does have the spirit of fear. I have tried to convince him that he can trade the one for the other, and that it's a can't-miss, sure-fire good deal. So far, he'd rather yank on that chain around his neck until he's blue in the face than trust in God.

THE WORK OF A LIFETIME

King Solomon apparently knew the fear of God, lost it somewhere along the line, and regained it toward the end of his life. It certainly took Jacob the lion's share of a lifetime to learn it. The fear of God isn't stamped out in a mold on an assembly line, and there's more than one way to learn it. The sooner we learn it the better, but it's never too late. We need to remember that God is more concerned with where we end up than where we started out.

To this point, we have seen that love casts out fear, and that the fear of God is a partnership between the believer and the Lord. In the next chapter, we will see how failure eventually produced the fear of God in a man and gave him the strength and courage to put his life on the line for his youngest brother. Judah was a man who learned the full meaning of the fear of God, both from the perspective of man and the Lord, and became a great patriarch in the line of the Messiah as a result. His story is of a man transformed from a rascal into a man of God, teaching that no matter what we started out as, God can elevate us to the greatest heights of righteousness through Jesus Christ.

CHAPTER 6

SON OF A RASCAL

J UDAH IS AN important character in the Bible, not only because he is in the bloodline of the Messiah, but also because he demonstrates how failure can refine a man like silver is refined in a furnace. The fear of failure, like actual failure itself, confronts us all throughout the course of our lives. No one enjoys failure but it is the inevitable outcome of being human. We have failed relationships, failed jobs, failed expectations, failed hopes, dreams, and ambitions. Our car may fail on the freeway, our bank account may fail when we need to make a rent payment, and even our health will fail us. Failure, fear, disappointments, and letdowns are as predictable as a puppy destroying a new carpet.

Examining Judah also helps us understand why the Bible contains some extremely sordid stories. In fact, that is a word that fairly describes Judah when we meet him for the first time in Genesis 37:26. As Jacob's fourth eldest son by Leah, it was his bright idea that instead of murdering their youngest brother, Joseph, they should sell him into slavery to the Ishmaelites so they could at least make some money. First impressions are important and Judah was off to a bad start.

Keep in mind that Jacob's three eldest sons had not particularly distinguished themselves up to this point, either. The eldest, Reuben, "went and lay with Bilhah his father's concubine" (Gen. 35:22), defiling Jacob's bed. Simeon and Levi, Jacob's second and third eldest sons, had unconscionably murdered every male in the town of Shalem, a city of Shechem, after their sister Dinah had been defiled (Gen. 34:25). It is not unreasonable at this point to call into question what kind of father Jacob had been, based on the behavior of his boys.

After Joseph is sold, all the boys conspire to lie to Jacob about how "an evil beast hath devoured" his youngest son (Gen. 37:33). Next, we meet up with Judah in Genesis 38, and if there's an uglier chapter in the Bible, short of the ones covering the Lord's crucifixion, we'd be hard-pressed to identify it. In this chapter, the Lord slays two of Judah's sons, Er and Onan, because they were wicked (Gen. 38:7–10). To make an ugly story short, Judah's wife dies, and his daughter-in-law dresses like a harlot to trick Judah because he wouldn't let her have his third youngest son in marriage to carry on the line of Er or Onan. Judah unwittingly picks her up by the side of the road, impregnates her, and she has twins. These are not the actions of a man who fears God.

It isn't going out on a limb to say Judah didn't start out as a great man. But by the grace of Jesus Christ he finished as a great man and that's what counts. Judah was set to have his daughter-in-law burned for playing the harlot and getting pregnant, until he learned he was the father. In Genesis 38:26, we hear Judah say something smart for the first time: "She hath been more righteous than I."

Somewhere between Genesis 38:26 and 44:16, Judah's soul must have been doing some Olympic-class wrestling with the spirit of God. Chapters 39–43 document the well-known story of Joseph's rise to prominence in Egypt as prime minister. Our focus of interest, however, is on the change of character that's evident in Judah as the result of God's dealing with him during this period of time. The old Judah in Genesis 38:26 is a different Judah than the one in 44:16, and the new one is an enormous improvement.

ANATOMY OF A HEART

Judah took after his father, and he was as much a rascal as Jacob was. But after some years of hard living Judah looked deep inside his soul and saw a leanness that made him ache for the cleansing spirit of God. At least twenty years had gone by since Joseph had been sold into slavery, and the Lord must have worked Judah over pretty good during that time. The daughter-in-law he got pregnant had twin boys; Pharez and Zerah, to remind him of the two wicked sons the Lord had taken away. Judah must have spent some lonely, painful time staring at the night, wondering where he had gone wrong. No doubt, his brother Joseph weighed heavy on his mind.

> But the hour cometh, and now is, when the true worshippers shall worship the Father in spirit and in truth: for the Father seeketh such to worship him. God is a

Spirit: and they that worship him must worship him in
spirit and in truth.

—JOHN 4:23–24

Judah had been in a foot race with his personal dragons
for a number of years and they finally caught up with him.
He either had to surrender and serve, or fight for the truth
in the spirit of the fear of God.

Some people wonder why those ugly episodes about
Judah are in the Bible, and other stories that may be worse
than that. We are given these stories so we may see the
changes that occur inside someone else's heart. It's like
those "before" and "after" pictures advertisers use to sell the
latest weight loss product. The lusts and desires of the flesh
are fairly easy to identify and describe, but the things of the
spirit aren't that simple. Things of the spirit come straight
from a person's heart, and they're sometimes easier to see
by their absence than by their presence.

Here's an example. Most people who have lived long
enough have seen someone they loved very dearly die
before their eyes, maybe in a hospital or a nursing home. Or,
maybe they have come across a loved one the next morning
and found them dead in bed. It is one of the most heart-
wrenching experiences anyone could ever have. You know
immediately the spirit of that person is gone, and you know
it with absolute finality. You can't explain it, it is beyond
comprehension, the emotion of grief seems inadequate, but
the certainty of it is the harshest reality there is.

God gives a living spirit to every human being. While
that person is alive they can worship in spirit and truth
in the fear of God, or they can throw cold water on the
spirit. People who do the latter may still be breathing, but
if they're spiritually dead they're only marginally better off
than someone who is stone-cold dead. That is where Judah

was. Jesus spoke about sinning and offending children in Mark 9:43–44. He said:

> If thy hand offend thee, cut it off: it is better for thee to enter into life maimed; than having two hands to go into hell, into the fire that never shall be quenched: Where their worm dieth not, and the fire is not quenched.

Judah was still alive and breathing, but he could feel the worm that wouldn't die eating away at him, and a hot fire in his belly that never went away. That is what sin does to a person's spirit if they don't face up to the truth and ask Jesus Christ for forgiveness, and that's where fear has its most fertile breeding ground.

We find Judah standing before the prime minister of Egypt in Genesis 44:16. Judah didn't realize the prime minister was his brother, Joseph. Until that time, Judah had done a pretty poor job of managing his life. He sold his youngest brother into slavery, and helped show Joseph's coat of many colors to his father, sprinkled with goat's blood, to convince the old man his favorite son was dead. Judah had raised two good-for-nothing sons so bad the Lord saw fit to slay them. It has been said when we get to heaven we will be surprised at some of the people who made it there, and we will also be surprised at some of the people who didn't. Suffice it to say no one should expect to see Er and Onan in heaven because those two boys were just plain wicked and no source of pride for Judah.

So, as Judah stood before the prime minister of Egypt with his youngest brother Benjamin's freedom on the line, he had every cause to be a humble man. We have to read between the lines, but Judah had reached his limit on sin. He had probably made more mistakes than the Bible tells us and they were weighing heavy on him. This was where he drew a line in the sand, overcame all his fears, and became a great man of faith, courage, and character. This point can't be stressed too strongly: we are not told about Judah's failings so we can wag our fingers at him and say what a disgrace he was. We are told about his failings in the flesh so we have a point of reference to observe his subsequent regeneration into a man of the spirit and a great man of God.

Judah volunteered to serve as Joseph's slave, but no doubt, he would have given up his life before returning home to Jacob without Benjamin. It is a good thing Joseph revealed himself when he did because otherwise, prime minister or not, there probably would have been bloodshed if someone had tried to put chains on Benjamin. Judah understood the fullness of the fear of God, from the perspective of man and God, and the love of God cast out all his fear. It gave him the same type of courage and strength that Jesus had as He suffered and died on the cross, and the depth of commitment that would allow a man to substitute his life for another.

Everyone is different, but there are certain specific sins, which if a person commits, they would be better off if God had struck them dead with lightning first. I don't know if that's true for you, but it is for me and it was for Judah. He would rather have had his body of flesh die than offend the spirit of truth that lived inside him.

> If any man see his brother sin a sin which is not unto death, he shall ask, and he shall give him life for them that sin not unto death. There is a sin unto death: I do not say that he shall pray for it.
>
> —1 John 5:16

If Judah had allowed Benjamin to be taken as a slave without offering up his own life as a substitute, that well may have been Judah's sin unto death, and in his spirit, he knew it.

Judah could have washed his hands of Benjamin but he didn't. He could have rationalized that since Benjamin had stolen the prime minister's silver cup (Gen. 44:12), anything that happened to him wasn't Judah's fault. Although he didn't know Benjamin hadn't really stolen the cup and the whole incident was a set-up, Judah was under no obligation to step up the way he did. There were three older brothers ahead of him who should have taken responsibility for Benjamin. No one would have blamed him for Benjamin's apparent mistake. But Judah's fear of God outweighed any concern he had for his own life, and he was ready to offer it up as a substitute and atonement for Benjamin.

Because God's grace and mercy outweigh His justice, Judah became a great patriarch in the bloodline of the Messiah. Like Christ, through the fear of God he was able and willing to suffer pain and humiliation, and set aside his fears and even his life for the soul of another he valued dearly. He provides a wonderful example of someone overcoming their weakness and fear to embrace love in the performance of God's will, an act of worship that can't be surpassed.

CHAPTER 7

WHAT DOES GOD REALLY THINK OF US?

The fear of the wicked, it shall come upon
him: but the desire of the righteous shall be
granted.

—PROVERBS 10:24

A s GOD-FEARING CHRISTIANS our goal is ultimately to "have the mind of Christ" (1 Cor. 2:16). Jesus Christ is our standard and we want to see ourselves as God sees us, not the way we wish we were. There is little point in fooling ourselves and pretending to be something we are not, because we certainly aren't going to trick God. We may be able to convince other people that we are pretty special and wonderful, but if we try pulling that with God, He will straighten us out in short-order.

Young Joseph thought he was pretty special with his coat of many colors and his dreams about his brethren bowing down to him. Any ideas he had about being special got lost when his eleven brothers pushed him into that pit and sold him as a slave (Gen. 37:28).

Haman thought he was indispensable to King Ahasuerus, who ruled the Medo-Persian Empire. In the Book of Esther, he conspired to have all the Jews in the Empire killed just because one of them, Mordecai, wouldn't bow down to him. God straightened Haman out on a gallows at the end of a rope (Esther 7:10).

King Hezekiah was sick unto death in 2 Kings 20, and he didn't think that was fair because he had been such a good king. God in His mercy gave Hezekiah another fifteen years to live, but if those fifteen years produced anything good, the Bible doesn't say what they were. He had a son named Manasseh during that time, who was one of the worst kings Judah ever had. "Manasseh made Judah and the inhabitants of Jerusalem to err, and to do worse than the heathen, whom the LORD had destroyed before the children of Israel" (2 Chron. 33:9). Then Hezekiah showed the son of the Babylonian king all the precious things of Judah. That boy must have made a list of everything he saw, and Isaiah prophesied to Hezekiah that everything would be carted off to Babylon, and it was. It was also prophesied that all of Hezekiah's sons would be hauled off to Babylon and turned into eunuchs. Hezekiah said that was fine with him, as long as there was "peace and truth" in his days (2 Kings 20:19). It may be surmised that some of the sons of Hezekiah lost their fondness for the king after that remark. Hezekiah was a great king who, if he had died on schedule, wouldn't have skunked up his legacy the way he did.

A Tough Assessment

> And GOD saw that the wickedness of man was great in the earth, and that every imagination of the thoughts

of his heart was only evil continually. And it repented the LORD that he had made man on the earth, and it grieved him at his heart.

—GENESIS 6:5–6

This verse refers to the people who lived prior to the time of the great flood. After the flood, Noah built God an altar and offered a sacrifice. The good news, at that point, is God promised not to "smite any more every thing living, as I have done" (Gen. 8:21). The bad news is His opinion of us hadn't changed much: "for the imagination of man's heart is evil from his youth" (Gen. 8:21).

I have taken the liberty to paraphrase these verses, along with Jeremiah 17:9 and Romans 7:18 into one verse as follows:

"There is no good thing in any imagination or thought of man's deceitful, desperately wicked heart, which is evil above all things from his youth, continually." (Paraphrase of Gen. 6:5–6; 8:21; Jer. 17:9; and Rom. 7:18).

These are not words God used in a moment of anger and wishes He could take back. He wasn't exaggerating, and it wasn't a case of words carelessly or poorly selected. These verses make no distinction between essentially good people, those who are a little wicked, and those who are completely wicked. He's talking about you and me.

God goes even further and says it "repented" and "grieved" Him that He created us. Perhaps it is best to understand what these words mean in context with a God who is omnipotent and omniscient, much like we understand the meaning of the fear of the Lord. After all, God doesn't make mistakes, and since He designed us He must have known how things would turn out and planned ahead for it. Our wickedness could not have come as a surprise to God, so the words *repented* and *grieved* must be interpreted in light of who He is and our limited ability to understand Him. Because God is omniscient and His eternal purpose can't be frustrated, *repented* and *grieved* must be defined within a scholarly theological framework.

So here it is: God was so deeply sickened by what He saw in man that He sorely regretted ever making us. If it weren't for His grace and Noah, God would have blotted us off the face of the earth the way you or I would scrape something disgusting off the bottom of our shoe. He was so disgusted by what He saw in the days of Noah, He flooded the entire planet, leaving only eight people to repopulate the earth. He could have used the planet Mars like a cue ball on a galactic pool table and bank-shot Earth off Mercury and directly into the sun, and would have been justified in doing so. Instead, He mercifully gave Himself to us as a Savior, for which we should be exceedingly grateful.

Speak for Yourself, Pal

Most people, Christians included, would reject this assessment of their character. "Evil continually" means "cranky once in a while," and "evil from his youth" means "I was a rotten kid, but that's all past." "Desperately wicked" refers to the other guy, and "no good thing" means "some good, some bad."

There is an old saying that if you knew me like I did you wouldn't want anything to do with me. But hold on, because if I knew you the way you know yourself, I wouldn't want anything to do with you, either, and then none of us would talk to each other. Most people operate under the self-assessment that they're warm, wonderful, considerate, and essentially good.

An important aspect to the fear of God is to acknowledge His assessment of us, recognize that it is different from ours, and to agree with Him. "The fear of the LORD is to hate evil: pride, and arrogancy, and the evil way, and the froward mouth, do I hate" (Prov. 8:13). God hates pride and arrogance, and in view of how He assesses us, who can blame Him? "By humility and the fear of the LORD are riches, and honour, and life" (Prov. 22:4). God wants us to be humble. At the risk of repetition, in view of His assessment of our condition, who can blame Him?

That is one of the reasons God gave us the Bible. It cleans us up and washes the dirt out of our minds and ears. It is reminiscent of Joshua the high priest in Zechariah 3, who was wearing filthy garments as he stood before the angel of the Lord, with Satan at his right hand. The angel of the Lord cleaned Joshua up and made him look good, and that is what the Holy Spirit and the Bible can do for us. It is impossible to walk out the front door in the morning and not get covered with the filth of the world, and the only One who can clean us, from the tip of our feet to behind our ears, is Jesus Christ.

We are free to reject God's assessment of our character, but that won't change it, nor will it be any less accurate simply because we disagree. If we aren't covered with the righteousness of Christ we are only "evil, continually." Because of what we are without Christ, it is highly predictable that our worst fears should come upon us. In fact, we may conclude that people without faith in Christ subject themselves to a level of fear and anxiety that at times can be overwhelming.

THE FRUITFUL USE OF FEAR

We can retain our pride and arrogance and reject God's assessment of our character if we choose. If that is our choice we should not be surprised when God chastises us.

51

"I also will choose their delusions, and will bring their fears upon them" (Isa. 66:4). God may choose to drop the hedge of protection that surrounds us if chastisement is in order and a lesson needs to be learned.

> Then Satan answered the LORD, and said, Doth Job fear God for nought? Hast not thou made an hedge about him, and about his house, and about all that he hath on every side? thou hast blessed the work of his hands, and his substance is increased in the land.
>
> —Job 1:9–10

There's a huge difference between a person who slays their fears and one who ignores them. The difference between someone who ignores their fears and an ignoramus is much closer. Fear from God, when it comes in the form of chastisement, is intended to evoke a response or change in behavior that will provide us with benefit. God's motive in chastising us is to bring us to repentance, to agree with Him, not for His sake, but for our own. Our fears need to be confronted head-on and evaluated to determine if they are the result of unrighteous living, and if so, a positive change by us will cause the fears to be alleviated.

Fixing What Is Broken

> But those things which proceed out of the mouth come forth from the heart; and they defile the man. For out of the heart proceed evil thoughts, murders, adulteries, fornications, thefts, false witness, blasphemies.
>
> —Matthew 15:18-19

These verses apply to everyone with a heart, and most of us fit in that category. Jesus describes some of the things that people think about each other for no good reason. They aren't just thinking them about me. They are also thinking them about you.

In James 3:8, the Lord's half-brother wrote, "But the tongue can no man tame; it is an unruly evil, full of deadly poison." The "heart" that Jesus refers to in Matthew 15, speaks of our innermost being, or soul, stripped naked of all pretension, vain conceit, and pride. It stands naked beneath a glaring light, with every spot, wrinkle, blemish, and stain exposed to the brightness of truth. The heart is who we are, motivating our thought processes, the way we think and the things we say. It is where wicked imaginations are generated, and we can either cleanse them with the Word of God, or allow them to plant roots that may blossom out of our mouth as venomous poison.

Not all the poison in our hearts and imagination finds expression in the tongue. Sometimes the mouth will clamp shut like a trap, preventing the wicked thought from escaping the lips. Some people are better than others at consistently keeping their wicked thoughts to themselves. However, no one is successful all the time. "If any man offend not in word, the same is a perfect man, and able also to bridle the whole body" (James 3:2). That doesn't sound like anyone I know.

"Even a fool, when he holdeth his peace, is counted wise: and he that shutteth his lips is esteemed a man of understanding" (Prov. 17:28). Now that is someone I can relate to. I must confess there have been times I have worked myself into a state of anger by allowing an overactive imagination to think the worst of other people without any reason or justification whatsoever. I have done it to family, friends, coworkers, and even to our dogs. I have actually gotten mad at our dogs by imagining they dig holes in the ground just to be ornery. If you were to say this is ridiculous, you would be right.

Evil thoughts can creep into our mind at any time of the day or night. Daydreaming provides fertile soil for less than wholesome thinking, and people do it while driving, before falling asleep, while performing tedious and repetitive tasks, and at many other times as well. There are some daydreams a God-fearing Christian ought not to have. For example, a Christian should not daydream about having sex with someone who is not their spouse. Jesus said in the Sermon on the Mount, Matthew 5:28, that to look at a woman with lust in your heart is sinful and, therefore, a sin. Job said in 31:1 "I made a covenant with mine eyes; why then should I think upon a maid?" Job trained himself not to stare at every beautiful woman he saw so he wouldn't have indecent thoughts. He was a man about whom God said, "There is none like him in the earth, a perfect and an upright man, one that feareth God, and escheweth evil" (Job 1:8). That is high praise for a God-fearing man.

There is no reason for a man to stare at a beautiful woman as though he can't control the direction of his gaze. The eyes are controlled by voluntary muscles, and we should refrain from letting them linger and leer over every square inch of a lady we don't even know. I enjoy looking at beautiful women just as much as the next guy, but there is a crossover point from natural appreciation to evil thought. When we deliberately allow ourselves to cross over then we have committed the sin Jesus spoke of. That is what happens when we constantly allow our thoughts to drift aimlessly and without deliberate purpose.

Christians should not daydream about winning the lottery so they can quit their job and take life easy. Playing the lottery in the first place probably isn't a terrific thing for Christians to do because they are relying on luck rather than Jesus. And even if they win, there are folks who hold the opinion that what they have won is dirty money, and I would be one of them. We should remember the rich fool of Luke 12. Even if we were rich God would still expect us to work. I know this all sounds a little prudish, but frankly I don't care and neither should you. We don't have to apologize for fearing God and being different from unbelievers. If we don't want to share the common fears of unbelievers, we can't afford to think like unbelievers.

The apostle Paul addressed the issue of evil thoughts and imaginations that come out of the heart in 2 Corinthians 10:3–5 and compares the subject to warfare.

> For though we walk in the flesh, we do not war after the flesh: (For the weapons of our warfare are not carnal, but mighty through God to the pulling down of strong holds;) Casting down imaginations, and every high thing that exalteth itself against the knowledge of God, and bringing into captivity every thought to the obedience of Christ.

The fear of God is to hate evil, and Jesus wants us to cast down (evil) imaginations, bringing into captivity every thought to the obedience of Christ. He wouldn't ask us to do something we are not capable of. We can never completely eliminate evil thoughts and imaginations: that kind of purity seems out of reach until after our resurrection. But we can certainly "cast down" such imaginations, as Paul says. We ought to be able to consciously and quickly recognize when our thoughts are going in a direction they shouldn't go, and cut them off or cast them down. When we realize an evil imagination has taken hold, the last thing we should do is let it run its course. We may have a lapse and want to kill someone, but we should repudiate ourselves immediately, not meditate on how we are going to pull off the crime and dispose of the murder weapon. A failure to cut short such an imagination would be a sin in accordance with Matthew 15:19, because it came from the heart and we didn't stop it when we had a chance. The Holy Spirit will clean those thoughts out if we look to Him for help, but we have to avert our gaze His way. "The wisdom that is from above is first pure, then peaceable, gentle, and easy to be intreated, full of mercy and good fruits, without partiality, and without hypocrisy" (James 3:17).

We should honestly evaluate our thought processes, and determine whether we engage in too many meaningless activities such as daydreaming. An honest assessment of daydreams will reveal they are of no value, and usually are not either positive or wholesome. They kill time when we are bored, but as Christians we should rarely be bored and not kill time because it is too precious. The Holy Spirit doesn't want us wasting our time daydreaming on nonsensical flights of fancy. With His help, meaningless and evil daydreams can be substantially reduced from our thought activities, and replaced with more productive, wholesome, and interesting spiritual matters.

> Finally, brethren, whatsoever things are true, whatsoever things are honest, whatsoever things are just, whatsoever things are pure, whatsoever things are lovely, whatsoever things are of good report, if there be any virtue, and if there be any praise, think on these things.
> —Philippians 4:8

> Let the words of my mouth, and the meditation of my heart, be acceptable in thy sight, O Lord.
> —Psalm 19:14

Paul speaks of "the pulling down of strongholds" in 2 Corinthians 10:4. We have those strongholds in our hearts and minds, and they are as formidable as any gated fort or garrison built of wood, stone, or brick. The walls are smooth so no one can climb them from the outside, too tall for any ladder, and thick enough to withstand battering rams. Strongholds are used to prevent unwanted things, like an enemy from getting in, but they may also keep out new ideas or fresh concepts we need in order to keep a balanced perspective. Strongholds may also keep things in like bigotry, lies, hatred, and other confusions of an evil imagination that poison our soul and spirit.

> These six things doth the LORD hate: yea, seven are an abomination unto him: A proud look, a lying tongue, and hands that shed innocent blood, An heart that deviseth wicked imaginations, feet that be swift in running to mischief, A false witness that speaketh lies, and he that soweth discord among brethren.
> —PROVERBS 6:16–19

Jesus lists seven things that come forth from the heart and defile a man in Matthew 15:19, and these verses from Proverbs list seven more that are an abomination. There's overlap, and if the list were consolidated it would contain a total of ten items. In addition to those listed in Matthew 15 would be added a proud look, feet swift in running to mischief, and sowing discord among brethren. All ten items require either spoken words or a physical action on the part of a person, with the exception of the devising of wicked imaginations. It is placed right alongside murder, theft, and lying, even though the only person who can "see" us think is God.

The penalty for a premeditated crime is always higher than a spontaneous criminal action because the criminal uses his wicked imagination to plan the crime. Job made a covenant with his eyes not to stare upon fair maidens, so it was pretty unlikely he would commit adultery. If a person is always daydreaming and fantasizing about having an affair with someone who is not their spouse, when the opportunity arises, and it will, that person is more likely to take the last fateful step and commit adultery. Their mind has been conditioned and prepared, making that last step a lot smaller than for a person who repudiates such impulses at every occurrence. In addition, a person who is always thinking about sex is more likely to have a wandering eye, thereby increasing the probability of temptation arising.

Divine Nature

God gave us a brain and He expects us to exercise it. If we always allow our mind to just lazily idle along, slowly spinning like a windmill that isn't attached to anything, evil thoughts and unnecessary fears will quickly overtake us. God tells us in 2 Peter 1:4–7 that He has shared with us His divine power to pull down strongholds and cast down wicked imaginations. Either we possess these promises through faith or they are empty platitudes.

> Whereby are given unto us exceeding great and precious promises: that by these ye might be partakers of the divine nature, having escaped the corruption that is in the world through lust. And beside this, giving all diligence, add to your faith virtue; and to virtue knowledge; And to knowledge temperance; and to temperance patience; and to patience godliness; And to godliness brotherly kindness; and to brotherly kindness charity.

If we contemplate these things, we will find less room for wicked imaginations to fill the vacuum in our minds. If we are lazy-brained we open the door for the dragons of our fear to come rushing in and create mind pollution. The cleansing power of the Word of God can rinse that pollution out, making room for the "divine nature" of Jesus Christ in our thinking and in our lives.

CHAPTER 8

STEERING CLEAR OF EVIL

The first of all the commandments is, Hear, O Israel; The Lord our God is one Lord: And thou shalt love the Lord thy God with all thy heart, and with all thy soul, and with all thy mind, and with all thy strength: this is the first commandment. And the second is like, namely this, Thou shalt love thy neighbour as thyself. There is none other commandment greater than these.

—MARK 12:29–31

A PARABLE OF CONTRAST

WHEN I WAS a child, an older kid in the neighborhood put me on a bicycle and pushed it down a hill. I fell off, but it was a long hill so he put me back on the bike and kept pushing it downhill until I stopped falling. He didn't give me any verbal instruction on how to stay balanced, there was no written test and he didn't put a hand on my shoulder to keep me steady. He just said he would beat me up if I didn't get on the bicycle and then would push it downhill.

I was less afraid of falling than I was of getting beat up, so I chose to get back on the bicycle. Eventually I learned the best way to avoid getting all skinned up was to stay balanced on the bicycle. I'm not certain what all the variables of staying balanced are, but I've never forgotten them. If you can explain in a meaningful way to a five-year-old child how to stay balanced on a bicycle, then maybe you can explain precisely which of God's commandments must be obeyed and which can be ignored. I can't do either one.

Since the bicycle story is a parable of contrast, the point to be made is that God is not like that kid who made me learn to stay balanced. I could fall off the bicycle by myself, and he didn't offer any help to keep me on except to push harder. He not only didn't provide any instruction, he also didn't care whether I was fearful or not. God does not want us to be fearful, and He's provided specific instructions in the Bible on how we are to lead balanced lives that will help us avoid fear and evil.

THROWING A MONKEY WRENCH INTO THE WORKS

We have discussed to this point the fear of God, and what it means both from the perspective of man and God. From our perspective, it means to agree with God and "hate evil." From God's perspective, it is a promise to pour out blessings of wisdom, knowledge, and freedom from evil. We know that God loves and protects His children, and that "there is no fear in love; but perfect love casteth out fear" (1 John 4:18). If we take these elements together with faith in Jesus Christ we can live lives free of fear, right?

Easier said than done. What specifically must we do to uphold our end of the bargain, that is, the part about hating evil? Other than the occasional Middle Eastern terrorist or the odd stateside mass murderer, most folks we come across on a daily basis appear to hate evil. Heaven is going to be mighty crowded if all the people who pretend to be Christians and to hate evil are going to be there.

If we want a more accurate picture of how many people are really going to be in heaven we might ask this question: "Do you believe that Jesus was crucified for your sins, died for your sins, and resurrected so that you may have eternal life through Christ as your Lord and Savior?" That will shorten the line at heaven's gate. Born-again Christians would have no trouble answering this question in the affirmative. We could ask another question based on the writings of King Solomon that would also separate the wheat from the chaff. Solomon told us "the conclusion of the whole matter: Fear God, and keep his commandments, for this is the whole duty of man" (Eccl. 12:13). How would most Christians respond when asked whether they measured up to Solomon's tasking to fear God and keep His commandments? Many would probably pause for a moment and think before answering, and it's unlikely every answer would be the same. Most answers would probably fall along the line of, "Hmmm, well, yes, for the most part, hmmm, yes but..."

Specifically, how does a person go about fearing God and hating evil so that we aren't beset by the unnatural fears and dread of the world? We demonstrate our hatred of evil by keeping God's commandments. They are given to us as a yardstick against which we may measure ourselves and evaluate our success or failure. But that isn't very specific, is it? After all, what does it mean to "keep God's commandments"? Those grouchy old Pharisees that crucified the Lord would probably have professed to fearing God and keeping His commandments, and most of them probably weren't saved. Besides, since we are in the dispensation of grace and not the law, we are not bound by a bunch of rules and regulations, right?

"If ye love me, keep my commandments" (John 14:15). In every Bible I have ever seen, the only person whose words are printed in red is You-Know-Who. John 14:15 is printed in red, so that means You-Know-Who expects us to keep His commandments. That kind of throws a monkey wrench into the theory that we are not bound by any laws. But don't worry, because it's a little monkey wrench and it's lightweight, so it isn't burdensome to carry around.

Tossing Fear Behind Our Back

The best way to leave fear behind is to hate evil, which means simply to obey God and stop sinning, with today being the best day to start. Every Christian has skeletons in their closet they have repented of but wish they could deep-six in 10,000 fathoms of water, never to see the light of day. There may or may not be anything that can be done about the skeletons that are already there, but I know in my case they have plenty of company and don't need any more. When we repent of past sins, and fix the things in our lives that we know are wrong, we have no reason to cast fretful gazes behind us, fearful that some lie or shenanigan is going to catch up to us.

Apparently, one of the advantages God has over us is that He doesn't remember the sins of those with faith in Christ. "I, even I, am he that blotteth out thy transgressions for mine own sake, and will not remember thy sins" (Isa. 43:25). God is holy and righteous and doesn't want to look on something that's unclean, like sin and sinners. When He looks at a Christian, for His own sake He sees Jesus, and who can blame Him? I wish I could look in a mirror and see Jesus, but it's always me, and if I get tired of looking at myself God can't feel any different. The difference is that He forgets my sins while I remember them the way you might remember somebody sticking an ice pick in your liver.

God has provided specific commandments that assist our quest to depart from evil so that we may participate in His divine purpose without being in bondage to fear. "Thou shalt have no other gods before me" (Exod. 20:3) was the first of the Ten Commandments Moses received from God and presented to the children of Israel, and contrary to evidence today it's still the first of the commandments. It was given to warn the children of Israel against idolatry, which is normally associated with people of ancient times bowing to statues of wood and stone, or worshiping gods of the sun, moon, and stars. This still occurs in some areas of the world today, but as human civilization has aged, many of the original forms of idolatry have been modified to reflect modern attitudes, values, and inventions like television.

"Master, which is the great commandment in the law? Jesus said unto him, Thou shalt love the Lord thy God with all thy heart, and with all thy soul, and with all thy mind. This is the first and great commandment" (Matt. 22:36–38). Loving something more than God, or worshiping the wrong god, opens the door to every form of sin the imagination of man can conceive. Loving God with all one's heart, soul, and mind acts as a firewall against idolatry, sin, and fear: if that wall is burned down nothing stands between a person's soul and the flames of hell. When the first and great commandment is broken or ignored, it sets in motion wholesale fear and unrepentant sin like a cascading chain of dominoes. The fear of God keeps that firewall intact, enabling us to stay in line with all other of God's commandments and not in bondage to the fears of the flesh.

Predetermination vs. Free Will— The Debate Settled

If you want to engage in debate about predetermination versus free will or faith versus works, you are free to do so. But I don't intend to argue with anyone about those issues because they aren't very interesting. If not being interested makes me a simpleton, I plead guilty. The issue is settled.

On a more practical level, we may consider whether all commands contained in the Bible can be considered logical derivatives of the two great commandments given by Jesus in Mark 12:29–31. In other words, if we obey the two great commandments do we have to worry about any of the others that are given, and if so, how many and which ones? In addition, because we are saved by faith through the grace of God, not by works or the keeping of the law, which if any commandments are we bound by? Since our objective is to overcome our fears, we have to be able to discern which of God's commandments we are subject to and which may not apply. If we are obeying the commandments of Jesus, we have nothing to fear.

Broadly speaking, the two great commandments encompass most if not all aspects of the Ten Commandments. The Ten Commandments were given to the children of Israel as part of the Mosaic Law, but represent God-given truth that is still relevant today. They provide more specificity regarding personal behavior toward God and other people than the two great commandments. When we get to the Sermon on the Mount, we find additional specificity added to the Ten Commandments. For example, Matthew 5:21–22 instructs that we are not to kill, but in addition we aren't even to be angry without cause at our brother. The way we think is now included in our standard of conduct.

At a later point in the Sermon on the Mount, Jesus says, "Take therefore no thought for the morrow: for the morrow shall take thought for the things of itself. Sufficient unto the day is the evil thereof" (Matt. 6:34). This is similar to Jesus' parable in Luke 12 about the rich man who enjoyed such a bountiful harvest that he was going to take it easy, "eat, drink, and be merry," not realizing God would require his soul that night. Or James 4:13–15, where we are told not to brag about our big plans for making money in the future because life is but a vapor, and subject to the will of God.

These examples arguably fall outside the great commandments given after "Hear O Israel" in Mark 12:29–31. In 1 Corinthians 11:5–6, Paul says every woman who prays or prophesies with her head uncovered should have her head shaved. In 2 John 1:9–10, John tells us that if a person doesn't properly abide in the doctrine of Christ to not even let them in our house. First Peter 5:8 teaches us to be sober and vigilant. There is a tremendous amount of additional information and guidance in the Bible that is substantive and of value. In some instances, such as the Book of Leviticus, there are various instructions and regulations regarding sacrificial offerings, health and sanitation, and sexual relations. Christians are certainly not bound by the sacrificial requirements, although we can study them for edification.

Leviticus 20:10 commands that adulterers be put to death, but in John 8:7 Jesus dismisses the Pharisees after they brought an adulteress to him, saying, "He that is without sin among you, let him first cast a stone at her." Nowhere in the New Testament, however, is the punishment for adultery explicitly lifted.

In Deuteronomy 17:16–17 God told the children of Israel when they entered the Promised Land that the king was not to multiply horses, wives, silver, or gold to himself. We saw earlier that King Solomon did not heed this advice. Most of us today are probably not in danger of this type of disobedience. The point to be made with these illustrations is that there is room for different dispensations, different interpretations, and different applications of biblical truth. The Bible does not offer an all-inclusive laundry list of do's and don'ts that govern our lives. We are supposed to love the Lord God "with all thy mind." We are not like an ostrich or some other animal which God has "deprived... of wisdom, neither hath he imparted to her understanding" (Job 39:17). Unlike animals, in addition to a soul and spirit God has given us a brain and He expects us to use it.

The best way to keep all the commandments of God is to know the Word of God. We should be like a piece of meat that has marinated in the refrigerator for several hours, so when you eat it every bite is flavorful and tasty. That is probably how Isaac's savory venison was that he thought Esau had cooked. Believers should be marinated in the Word of God so we can use our minds, look to the Spirit for guidance, meditate on the Bible for edification, and think on our feet when we are faced with a new or unusual situation. The Bible isn't like one of those *Haynes Repair Manuals* you buy at an auto parts store that tells you step-by-step how to fix your car. Those manuals tell you how to replace the brake liners or an alternator, but using the Bible to fix a broken relationship or to live in strong confidence free from fear takes study, meditation, and divine guidance.

There is simply no substitute for Bible study if we want to steer clear of evil and fear in our lives. We are not talking about one of those condensed versions of the Bible you can buy in Barnes and Noble. They have "The Complete Idiot's Guide" to the Bible/Learning Spanish/Playing the Guitar/Computers/Performing Brain Surgery, etc., but that is not what we are talking about here. The only place we can go to learn God's commandments is the Bible, and because of its easy availability we make a mistake if we rely on someone else to tell us what it means.

The parable of contrast at the beginning of this chapter is intended to teach that some things, such as riding a bicycle, must be learned through experience. As long as the child gets on the bicycle, he will eventually figure out how to stay balanced. Keeping God's commandments, gaining mastery over fear, and finding the Lord's will for our lives is much the same. We may not be able to explain all the details of how it's done, but if we don't study the Bible for ourselves we will never learn.

CHAPTER 9

CHAOS AND BRAZILIAN BUTTERFLIES

Remove not the ancient landmark, which thy
fathers have set.

— PROVERBS 22:28

IMAGINE THIS HEADLINE in your local paper:

**Death Toll Rises On Eastern Seaboard
Brazilian Butterfly Causes Widespread
Devastation**

Ed Lorenz was a meteorologist at the Massachusetts
Institute of Technology in 1961. Using math and a computer, he ran a predictive model on air movements in the
atmosphere. In one of these runs he entered some erroneous
information into the computer that was off by about one-
one thousandth of a percent. He thought this small error
would have minimal effect so he continued with the model.

Much to his surprise, he found the small error changed the prediction enormously.

His weather study revealed that a very small, almost infinitesimal change in the starting conditions would dramatically change the end result in a very sensitive system. He named the phenomenon "the butterfly effect" to describe a system, in this case the weather, so sensitive that a butterfly flapping its wings in Brazil could cause a hurricane in New York.[1] When a hurricane hits New York and shuts everything down, we refer to that as chaos. The point is that unless every conceivable variable in an extremely complicated system can be identified with infinite and precise accuracy then a prediction will probably be wrong. If we are unable to accurately identify every variable in a system, from our perspective that system is chaotic.

If a gallon bucket of jelly beans is thrown in the air, we could say the jelly beans fall randomly or chaotically. The fact is, however, every single jelly bean lands precisely where it is supposed to based on initial relative position, velocity, trajectory, mid-air collisions, air currents, density, terrain of the floor, and a host of other variables. We can't predict where they all will land, but God could if He chose to. Just because we can't identify or predict which butterfly in Brazil caused the hurricane in New York doesn't mean God can't, if He chooses.

In Luke 13:4–5, Jesus says, "Or those eighteen, upon whom the tower in Siloam fell, and slew them, think ye that they were sinners above all men that dwelt in Jerusalem? I tell you, Nay: but except ye repent, ye shall all likewise perish."

On September 11, 2001, over three thousand people died in a horrific terrorist attack. The same question Jesus asked about the tower in Siloam may be asked in that case as well. There were certainly many God-fearing men and women who died on 9/11. We don't know why they died, but God does, and no doubt His outstretched arm received many that day. Those people, believers and unbelievers alike, didn't die randomly, subject to the flip of a coin or spilled out on the floor like a bunch of jelly beans. We don't know with absolute precision all the infinite variables of the ruined and lost lives, but God does.

Believers can take comfort in knowing that God has calculated the infinite variables in our lives and organized them for our benefit. If we love God with all our heart, mind, and soul and seek to implement His plan for our lives, we have no need to fear the stray arrows of chance striking us and turning our lives upside down. If there is an arrow with our name on it, we can be certain it was delivered to us from the hand of God, and there's a lesson in it for us. It may be a hard lesson and we might not like it, but because it's from God the only thing we have to fear is not getting the message He's sending us.

ANCIENT LANDMARKS, UNSHAKEABLE TRUTHS, RANDOM DISASTERS

The Word of God has some very specific things to say about certain kinds of behavior. God-fearing, born-again Christians should strive that their behavior and worldview are as much in line with the Bible as possible. We should not be surprised that when we flagrantly disregard specific instruction contained in God's Word we are visited with the spirit of fear. That is a certain and predictable outcome, and there is no way to state that fact gently. When we invite the dragon of fear to hop aboard our shoulders by willfully disobeying God's Word, he will jump on and weigh us down like a load of bricks. If we do that, we shouldn't whine and moan like a crybaby, expecting God to heal us while we are sticking Him in the eye with our finger.

God has prohibited certain behaviors and we are free to argue with Him about them if we choose. He gave us those prohibitions because He doesn't want any unintended "butterfly effects" throwing our lives or the lives of others into shambles. For example, Leviticus 18:22 states, "Thou shalt not lie with mankind, as with womankind: it is abomination." This is clearly a reference to the sin of homosexuality. God feels the same way about enchanters, witches, charmers, and consulters with familiar spirits. "For all that do these things are an abomination unto the LORD" (Deut. 18:12). God is not capricious and He doesn't pick on one group of people. He is unlikely, however, to surrender His sovereignty anytime soon.

There are many people who become very angry with those who hold the biblical view that homosexuality is an abomination. Such Christians are called mean-spirited, bigoted, hateful, homophobic, intolerant, and a host of other names. It can be very difficult to discuss some of these issues without getting emotional, upset, or angry. Plunging forward nonetheless, let's take Leviticus 18:22 one verse further: "Neither shalt thou lie with any beast to defile thyself therewith: neither shall any woman stand before a beast to lie down thereto: it is confusion" (Lev. 18:23).

For purposes of this discussion the most important part of Leviticus 18:22–23 are the last three words: "it is confusion." We should note that God doesn't explain in Leviticus why such behavior "is confusion"; He simply states it as a fact. God-fearing Christians are simply expected to trust that God knows what He is talking about when He says "it is confusion." If we try to explain why some behaviors are an abomination, going beyond the fact that it is sovereign God who has defined it, we join in the confusion. In other words, if we argue over something foolish we'll probably wind up looking like a fool.

God doesn't say homosexual couples can't have children through natural means, and can't raise children as effectively as a man and a woman in a traditional marriage. He offers no distinction between traditional marriage on the one hand, and same-sex marriages, or civil unions between homosexual partners on the other. He doesn't quote statistics of families broken apart by adultery, or the difficulties of raising a child in an out-of-wedlock birth to discourage promiscuity. Neither does He say drunks will die of cirrhosis of the liver or prostitutes will spread disease. In fact, nowhere in the Bible does God give us specific reasons why we are not supposed to steal. He only says, "Thou shalt not steal" (Exod. 20:15), and leaves it at that. Since God doesn't always go into specific detail explaining why certain behaviors cause confusion there is no reason we should. In fact, we should follow God's lead as much as possible.

When we were children, our parents would tell us to clean up our rooms. If I were to ask my parents why, I would likely have gotten one of two answers, or both. The first answer would have been, "Because I said so," and the second answer would have been a spanking. The same holds true for children who are told not to play with matches. You don't explain to them that the premium on your homeowner's insurance policy will go up if they burn the house down, or that you will have to buy a new wardrobe and live in a hotel for a month until you find another place to stay. You tell the child not to play with matches so they don't get burned, and don't play with matches because you said so. And you may even give the child a spanking as a down payment on the next time you catch him with matches.

Sometimes parents don't give their children all the whys

and wherefores on certain things, they just expect to be obeyed. No parent enjoys having a child challenge their authority, and no parent feels it's necessary to explain every detailed reason for every rule laid down. No parent appreciates a child who gets sassy and starts talking back, as though the child knows best and the adult is ignorant. God is no different. If we allow ourselves to become enmeshed in debate on behavior God has prohibited, and because He hasn't provided all the detailed consequences, we will eventually wind up arguing from a position of self-righteousness.

When we rely on our worldly skills of logic, reason, and experience to influence someone away from behavior that is flagrantly in rebellion against God we are unlikely to be persuasive. The fact is that nowhere in the Bible has God directed Christians to justify His judgments to anyone, or explain in precise analytical detail why His judgments are always right. Neither has He directed us to encourage vigorous debate on whether He has sovereign authority to make His judgments, and whether His judgments possess meritorious value. When we use temporal arguments of the flesh to convict someone else of sin in order to justify God "it is confusion" (Lev. 18:23) made worse by our vain and self-righteous attempts at persuasion. We would serve our witness better by stating quietly and confidently that, although we don't have all the answers, God's judgment has never been known to fall short in any matter and He has never disappointed us. In other words, if we find ourselves justifying God and His judgments to someone else we ought to consider for a moment how we got in that situation and whether or not we want to stay there.

We should have no fear or frustration when our testimony of Jesus Christ has small impact on those who are difficult or impossible to persuade. It is also worth noting that nowhere in the Bible has God required us to twist someone's arm until they cry "Uncle!" to believe as we do. As a Christian, however, He does require us to act as watchmen. If we see a sword coming upon the land, which as a figure of speech represents the Word of God and His judgment on those who are disobedient, we have to "blow the trumpet, and warn the people" (Ezek. 33:3). God doesn't tell us to blow the trumpet and then get into a fight with someone about why we blew it. We have to blow the trumpet loud enough and long enough, and then our task is done.

Moving ancient landmarks brings unintended consequences. God warns us to leave them alone not because He is mean and wants to restrict our freedom, but for our benefit and protection. We are not able to fully appreciate all the conditions and unknown variables that caused them to be placed in the first place. It is unwise to assume that a landmark or tradition was placed by someone less intelligent or sophisticated than we are. When we ignore their efforts and tamper with their work we run the risk of repeating mistakes they intended us to avoid.

When we move ancient landmarks, it sets in motion a chain reaction of events over which we have no control. It is like the kind of Rube Goldberg system Wile E. Coyote would use to try to catch Roadrunner. It has about twenty interdependent movable parts, each which must be sequentially triggered in a domino-like effect, with the net result that Roadrunner is supposed to be crushed underneath a load of bricks. Homosexuality, witchcraft, and other behaviors that willfully ignore and relocate God's ancient landmarks are like that contraption. It never works quite the way it is supposed to and the coyote is always a victim of his own clever invention.

No Fear

As He did for Adam in the Garden of Eden, God has provided boundaries for our benefit. They are based on God's ability to calculate the infinite variables, such as a butterfly flapping its wings in Brazil, and the consequences that result to us and others when boundaries are violated.

Our acts of rebellion may have unintended deleterious effects on other people that we can't see, or don't care about. The fact that we can't see or don't care if someone else gets hurt, however, doesn't mean God doesn't do both. He both sees and cares, and that gives Him the sovereign right to make the rules. God won't find fault with any of us because we come short of His omnipotence, but He may well place us in the balance and take our measure for not giving a hoot about the people we bring harm to.

When we reject God or fail to put our full trust and confidence in Him, we must, by default, settle for less than His best for our lives, and that includes being subject to unnatural fears and confusion. We also make ourselves a broader target for the stray arrows of disaster that may turn our lives upside down when we step off God's playing field and out of bounds. Implicit in the fear of the Lord is the simple wisdom that when God warns us of certain things He has a good reason, and we should heed that warning for our benefit. Regrettably, that is not the prevailing attitude in much of our world today.

CHAPTER 10

THE ENEMY WITHIN

I also will choose their delusions, and will bring
their fears upon them; because when I called,
none did answer; when I spake, they did not
hear: but they did evil before mine eyes, and
chose that in which I delighted not.

—ISAIAH 66:4

W E'VE ALL KNOWN people whose lives are always
spiraling out of control like a bad soap opera. I
know a woman who is always having financial
problems, marital problems, health problems, boyfriend
problems, and drug abuse problems all at the same time. She
thinks she is going to solve her financial problems by praying
to a little shrine she has in her home of Judas, of all people.
I don't know where she got that idea from and she doesn't
either, but that doesn't stop her from praying to it. Fast for-
warding through her marital, health, and boyfriend problems,
she is always popping Valium or one of those other name-
brand happy pills because she gets depressed. She is always
fearful, and rightfully so because her worst fears usually do

materialize. She has no interest in the things of Christ, and is only concerned with her appearance and driving a fancy car.

She is a very sad and unhappy person who fails to realize that every time she has gotten herself into a fix it has been her fault. In the last chapter, we talked about a butterfly causing a hurricane in New York. We can cause hurricanes in our lives as well because a little butterfly can morph into a dragon and wreak havoc with our fears. That is what happens to this woman I'm describing. For someone on the outside looking in, the difficulties she is experiencing are very predictable. From the inside looking out, the view obviously is much different, which is true for all of us.

My wife and I have tried to get through to her without much success. Her problems are certainly not insurmountable, for "There hath no temptation taken you but such as is common to man" (1 Cor. 10:13). Plenty of folks have beaten drug addictions, and the solution to her shrine of Judas is as close as the nearest trash can. Another problem she has is that she has no mountains to climb, no worthy challenges set before her to overcome, no ambition to do anything in service to God or anyone else besides herself. She is completely unable to recognize the cause-and-effect relationship between her sinful behavior and the problems she experiences, as though one had nothing to do with the other.

A Grim Tale

> In those days there was no king in Israel: every man did that which was right in his own eyes.
> — Judges 21:25

Justifying indefensible behavior is a sure way to bring dreadful, unnatural fear into our lives like a flood. It is the polar opposite of repentance and forgiveness of sins, and God hates it when we do it. When it becomes acceptable to justify aberrant behavior then restraint on all wickedness and evil is removed. Terrorists justify murdering their victims, activists justify aborting fetuses, adulterers blame their spouses for their own infidelity, and there is no depth of blackness the human heart can't reach. There is no reprobate behavior that someone without the fear of God can't persuasively justify.

That brings us to Judges 19–21, three of the darkest biblical chapters we can find. God gives us these horrible chapters in the hope we won't sink to the same level of depravity as the children of Israel during the time of Judges. These chapters are important to our examination of fear because they teach us something about our greatest adversary, the one we see in the mirror each morning. Our fears can never be overcome until we understand who is responsible for them, and it isn't God.

These chapters in Judges bear an eerie resemblance to the events leading up to the destruction of Sodom and Gomorrah. In this case, it is a Levite priest and his concubine passing through Gibeah, as opposed to the two angels who stay with Lot in Sodom. Like the men of Sodom, the men in Gibeah, who belonged to the tribe of Benjamin, wanted to have sex with the Levite priest, but they had to settle for the priest's concubine. The concubine was raped multiple times, murdered, and left on the threshold of the house the priest was staying at. The priest carried the dead woman home on a mule, chopped her body up into twelve pieces, and sent one piece to each of the tribes of Israel. The reader is left to ponder the apparently unsympathetic and unloving Levite priest who would allow his concubine to be so shamelessly treated, and then dismember her after her murder. He went to great lengths to persuade her to return with him to Mount Ephraim, suggesting some depth of emotional attachment. It isn't unreasonable to expect that, although he kept her as a concubine, he may have loved her. We aren't told how he sent her severed body parts throughout Israel, but since they didn't have Federal Express or refrigerated shipping in those days, we can surmise the package they arrived in was quite unpleasant.

The children of Israel were shocked and outraged, but apparently not at the Levite priest. They demanded the children of Benjamin deliver up the guilty men who had raped and murdered the concubine. The children of Benjamin refused and the stage was set for war.

We are not told specifically why the children of Benjamin refused to turn over the men of Gibeah that had acted so reprehensibly. Like the two angels in Sodom, the Levite was simply passing through Gibeah, and an old man coming in from his work offered the priest and his concubine hospitality, as was the custom of the day. For the men of Gibeah to demand sex with the priest was to repeat the crime of the Sodomites that resulted in their city's destruction by "brimstone and fire from the LORD out of heaven" (Gen. 19:24). There's no doubt whatsoever that every Israelite knew the story of the destruction of Sodom and Gomorrah, and it was utterly wicked for the children of Benjamin to defend the men of Gibeah. But somehow they found a way to justify their actions.

As we read further we learn the children of Israel weren't much better than the children of Benjamin. As they prepared to make war on Benjamin at the city of Gibeah, the children of Israel asked counsel of God. They asked, "Which of us shall go up first to the battle against the children of Benjamin? And the LORD said, Judah shall go up first" (Judg.

20:18). It turns out what God didn't say was very important because He didn't promise Judah they would win. In fact, the children of Israel lost 22,000 men that day to the tribe of Benjamin.

At this point, if the children of Israel had surmised God was not pleased with them, they would have been right. They whined and cried and licked their wounds, lined up again in battle formation, and presumptuously went back to seek counsel of God. They asked, "Shall I go up again to battle against the children of Benjamin my brother? And the LORD said, Go up against him" (Judg. 20:23). Now at this time a good question that someone should have asked, but no one did, would have been, "But Lord, will we win? Will You deliver them into our hand?" Since the question wasn't asked, I'm not going to speculate on what the answer would have been, but the result of that day's battle was another defeat for the children of Israel and 18,000 dead.

This is a good illustration of the way God dispenses justice. The same method was used against Israel when Nebuchadnezzar of Babylon destroyed Jerusalem and "Judah was carried away out of their land" (2 Kings 25:21). The prophet Habakkuk asked God, "Wherefore lookest thou upon them that deal treacherously, and holdest thy tongue when the wicked devoureth the man that is more righteous than he?" (Hab. 1:13). The answer to this question is God sometimes uses the very wicked to punish the less wicked. That doesn't mean the very wicked won't receive justice. They will, according to God's timetable. Very wicked Babylon was used to punish less wicked Judah, but Babylon wound up getting blotted off the face of the earth while Israel is with us to this day.

That is what was happening at Gibeah in Judges 20. God was displeased with the whole house of Israel because "every man did that which was right in his own eyes" (Judg. 21:25). The fear of God was the furthest thing from their minds. Both sides were self-righteous hypocrites who did nothing to bring glory to the name of the Lord. God sat back and let those two armies hack away at each other until both sides were bruised and bloody, just to make sure neither side won anything.

Before the children of Israel could subdue the tribe of Benjamin, they were required to demonstrate a little humility. After their second defeat they whined and cried and licked their wounds, but they also fasted and offered burnt offerings and peace offerings, and they may have even prayed a little.

> And Phinehas, the son of Eleazar, the son of Aaron, stood before it [the ark of the covenant] in those days,) saying, Shall I yet again go out to battle against the children of Benjamin my brother, or shall I cease? And the LORD said, Go up; for tomorrow I will deliver them into thine hand.
>
> —JUDGES 20:28

That day the children of Israel destroyed practically the entire tribe of Benjamin, killing 25,000 men.

LOSERS ALL AROUND

This story would have been bad enough had it ended at this point, but unfortunately, the Book of Judges has one chapter remaining. Fresh off their hollow victory at the city of Gibeah, the children of Israel went through the remaining cities of Benjamin, burned them, and killed all the men. Finally, feeling somewhat remorseful, the children of Israel decided to spare a handful of men from Benjamin in order to avoid that tribe's extinction. That was probably a good idea, but the method they chose to do so was as horrible as anything Benjamin had done. In order to get wives for these men, they murdered all the inhabitants of Jabash-gilead with the exception of 400 young virgins. The residents of Jabash-gilead were chosen because they had not supported the children of Israel in their fight with the tribe of Benjamin at Gibeah. We aren't told why the people of Jabash-gilead didn't fight, but it may be they wanted nothing to do with either side. Whatever the reason, they were ruthlessly murdered, and their virgins given to the remaining men of the Benjaminites.

They were still short a few virgins for the remaining men, however. The children of Israel solved this problem by having the Benjaminites who still needed wives kidnap them. "Behold, there is a feast of the LORD in Shiloh yearly in a place which is on the north side of Bethel" (Judg. 21:19). The remaining men kidnapped some of the women at the feast, took them back to the land of Benjamin, and rebuilt their cities. If this were a fairy tale you were telling your child at bedtime, you probably wouldn't be able to convince them that everyone lived happily ever after. Unfortunately it isn't a fairy tale, and one wonders how well the newlywed husbands slept at night, or whether they had to remove all sharp objects from inside the house. They may have feared their wives more than they feared God. The Book of Judges does not end happily, but happily, it does come to an end.

DEFENDING THE JUSTIFIABLE

No person who fears God would try to justify the behavior of the children of Israel or Benjamin as it is documented in Judges 19–21. They may have been forgiven later, and they may have been justified later, but only through the grace of God. They would not have been forgiven or justified if they

85

failed to repent and to agree with God regarding the sinfulness of their behavior.

"Therefore by the deeds of the law there shall no flesh be justified in his sight" (Rom. 3:20). You have heard that justification means it is "just-as-if-I'd" never sinned in the eyes of God. It is important to recognize who the source of justification is, and in whose eyes we are justified. Be assured it isn't you or me. I could tell you all day long you were justified in my eyes, but why in the world would you care? It's God's opinion you have to be worried about, not mine.

> Therefore as by the offence of one judgment came upon all men to condemnation; even so by the righteousness of one the free gift came upon all men unto justification of life. For as by one man's disobedience many were made sinners, so by the obedience of one shall many be made righteous.
> —ROMANS 5:18–19

It is through the obedience of Jesus Christ that we are justified in the eyes of God and made righteous. It is the grace of God that makes the righteousness of Christ available to us, not our hard work or keen intellect. "Not having mine own righteousness, which is of the law, but that which is through the faith of Christ, the righteousness which is of God by faith" (Phil. 3:9). If we make excuses for ourselves when we sin and rely on our own righteousness for justification, we are going to have a long, hard road to follow, and fear will be around every corner.

PURE AS THE WIND-DRIVEN SNOW

When the children of Israel waged war against the tribe of Benjamin both sides, absent the fear of God, were justified in their own minds. The problem was, they weren't justified in God's mind. The children of Israel had no righteousness of their own, as demonstrated by the way they murdered the inhabitants of Jabash-gilead and kidnapped the virgins of Shiloh. They were as bad as the children of Benjamin. Both sides justified indefensible behavior, making forgiveness and intercession with God impossible.

If someone is going to act as an intercessor for us with God, that person has to be better than we are. He has to have access to the holy of holies, be righteous in the eyes of God, and be able to impute that righteousness to us. The only One fitting that description is Jesus Christ, and the reason He measures up is because He is the Son of God, God the Son. "For all have sinned, and come short of the glory of God" (Rom. 3:23), except for Jesus Christ.

Martin Luther compared human beings to a pile of dung, but the righteousness of Christ covers the pile like a layer of freshly fallen snow. Some folks disagree with this assessment of the human condition. They contend the righteousness of Christ transforms the entire dung pile into a snow pile. If you pushed a rod through the middle of the pile only snow would stick to the sides. Because I know myself pretty well, I must regrettably conclude Luther is right and the "pure snow pile" folks are wrong.

When we fear God, we recognize His sovereignty, and His right to draw the boundaries of sin and righteousness. We must also recognize that when He offers salvation through Jesus Christ it is a "take-it or leave-it" proposition. If we don't play by His rules and repent of our sins He throws us out of the game. That is what happened to Korah of the tribe of Levi when he challenged Moses' authority and Aaron as high priest.

> And the earth opened her mouth, and swallowed them up, and their houses, and all the men that appertained

unto Korah, and all their goods. They, and all that appertained to them, went down alive into the pit, and the earth closed upon them: and they perished from among the congregation.

—NUMBERS 16:32–33

We will all receive commensurate with our faith. Those who look to Christ in faith for salvation and repent will receive eternal fellowship with God. Those who are embittered and cynical and expect nothing will receive it. Those who fear God and have faith in the glory of Jesus Christ will receive it abundantly, while those with faith in eternal gloom and despair will receive that in full measure. Everyone will receive according to their choice, but not everyone will be happy with what they receive.

The great flood of Noah's day is past, but man is still drowning in sin and many refuse to admit it. Like the woman we talked about at the beginning of this chapter, they conclude they aren't sinners and will justify any behavior, no matter how reprobate. They don't need or want a Savior and refuse to show God the fear and respect that is due Him. Someone drowning in sin doesn't have the option of choosing his or her rescuer; neither do we have the option of choosing our Savior. God has already made that decision for us. Those who refuse to accept His gracious offer and admit they are drowning will sink to the bottom faster than the apostle Peter did when he tried walking on water (Matt. 14:30).

CHAPTER 11

DIRTY WATER

Ye are of your father the devil, and the lusts
of your father ye will do. He was a murderer
from the beginning, and abode not in the
truth, because there is no truth in him. When
he speaketh a lie, he speaketh of his own: for
he is a liar, and the father of it.

—JOHN 8:44

J ESUS SPOKE THESE words to some Pharisees, and it is
impossible to characterize the statement as a gentle
rebuke or mild criticism. To use an old expression, we
could say the Son of God brought all guns to bear on those
hypocrites and fired for effect. These aren't the words of
some 1960s love child with flowers in his hair and a peace
symbol hanging around his neck. These are the words of the
Son of God, and those Pharisees probably felt like they had
been cracked over the head with a two-by-four.

There is no doubt our "adversary the devil, as a roaring
lion, walketh about, seeking whom he may devour" (1 Pet.
5:8). While recognizing that some of these subjects aren't
particularly cheery and uplifting to discuss, if we want to

lead joyful, Christ-centered lives free from bondage to natural fears, we need to understand the different sources of these fears. We can be certain our fears don't come about because of something God has done wrong. It is pointless to blame Satan for our fears because God has provided us the tools we need to overcome him through Jesus and the Word of God. So who does that leave to blame? Don't look at me because it isn't my fault, either.

Lying has become an inseparable part of the fabric of our society. It is the mechanism whereby sinful behavior is often justified, as we discussed in the last chapter. Whether lying has always been this prevalent in the past, or whether it has gotten worse recently, is difficult to gauge. It may be that as we age and grow more mature, we notice things that bother or upset us, which we might have overlooked when we were younger. It is impossible to assume an unbiased, consistent perspective when trying to evaluate a concept that can't be quantitatively analyzed. Do politicians lie more today than they did twenty or thirty years ago? Who's to say?

Naked Lies

Lies are corrosive, and cause tangible, long-lasting, or even sometimes permanent damage. The first lie in recorded history was told by Satan to Eve in Genesis 3:4, when he told her, "Ye shall not surely die," if she ate of the forbidden fruit. That lie had an effect that is with us today. After getting caught Adam told God he "was afraid, because [he] was naked" (Gen. 3:10). Unfortunately, he wasn't afraid before he ate the fruit. It wouldn't be fair to place the blame for the fall of man solely on Adam's shoulders. If Adam hadn't eaten the fruit, and everyone else in the intervening years had been obedient, I would have come along and messed things up for everybody. I don't expect to blister Adam with criticism when I meet him in heaven for causing all this trouble.

Some people seem to think lies are useful tools for achieving a purpose, and are only consequential when exposed. The fear of getting caught, while real, is not synonymous with the fear of God. Acts 5 tells of the consequences to Ananias and Sapphira, who paid with their lives for lying to the Holy Ghost. We can rest assured there won't be any lies told in new Jerusalem. "And there shall in no wise enter into it any thing that defileth, neither whatsoever worketh abomination, or maketh a lie: but they which are written in the Lamb's book of life" (Rev. 21:27).

Lies can and do kill. The unnamed man of God learned this truth in 1 Kings 13. He cried against the altar to Jeroboam, and was returning home by a different route than he had come, as the Lord had instructed him. He was also told to eat no bread or water, but the old prophet in Bethel, also unnamed, lied to the man of God and persuaded him to eat. The man of God believed the old prophet, and was killed by a lion on his way home as a result. This is one of those somewhat puzzling stories we often find in the Bible. The old prophet who lied didn't receive any punishment that we are told of, but the man of God who believed the lie paid with his life. The Bible doesn't tell us why the man of God was to return home by a different route, and wasn't allowed to eat or drink. It only tells us what happened when he believed another man's lie.

A lie helped destroy the relationship between Adam and God in the Garden of Eden. When Jacob lied and stole Esau's blessing from Isaac, the relationship between the two brothers was severely damaged. In 1 Kings 21, Jezebel conspired with lies to murder Naboth and steal his vineyard.

The conspiracy worked, but Jezebel paid with her life, and dogs ate her corpse. Gehazi, the servant of Elisha, became a leper as a result of his lie (2 Kings 5:27).

Charting Our Fate by the Words We Use

Lies destroy lives, relationships, and reputations. They cause us to fear unnecessarily, and prevent us from meeting challenges that will make us stronger once they have been overcome. The story of the twelve spies in Numbers 13 and 14 shows the powerful effect lies had in charting the destiny of the children of Israel. Those who told the lies, and those who believed the lies, both paid a heavy price.

What is particularly interesting about the story of the spies is the relationship between lies as spoken words, and the blessings or curses that may follow. After scouting out the Promised Land for forty days, the twelve spies returned to Moses with their report. Ten of the spies said, "We be not able to go up against the people [who inhabited the land]; for they are stronger than we" (Num. 13:31). They also slandered the Lord, saying, "Wherefore hath the LORD brought us unto this land, to fall by the sword, that our wives and our children should be a prey?" (Num. 14:3). They pronounced a "slander upon the land" (Num. 14:36) in an attempt to mischaracterize God's intentions and the good land He had given them.

As it turns out, the ten spies were actually telling a partial truth. When they said they couldn't go up against the inhabitants of the land because they were too strong, God agreed with them. They couldn't go into the land because they "died by the plague before the LORD" (Num. 14:37) for bringing back an evil report. On the other hand, Joshua the son of Nun and Caleb the son of Jephunneh were the only two spies that brought back an accurate report. Caleb said, "Let us go up at once, and possess it; for we are well able to overcome it" (Num. 13:30). God agreed with Caleb as well, and both Joshua and Caleb did enter the land, forty years later.

God was actually quite agreeable that day. He allowed all twelve of the spies to determine their fate by the words they chose to use. Those who didn't think they could enter the land were right, and those who believed they could enter the land were also right.

This story shows the powerful impact of words spoken honestly in contrast to words spoken dishonestly. It also shows the difference between faith and a lack of faith, and those who fear God and those who don't. Everyone who has ever witnessed to an unbeliever has heard them say something to the effect of, "I can't bring myself to believe in God." That person has spoken words that become reality and set their destiny, because God will agree with them. The only thing that prevents that person from starting off on a life of faith and fellowship with Jesus Christ is the difference between "can" and "can't." That difference amounts to one apostrophe and one small "t." "O taste and see that the LORD is good: blessed is the man that trusteth in him" (Ps. 34:8).

Unbelievers assume gravity will work as well tomorrow as it has today, and that the sun will rise in the morning. But they can't seem to change their mind-set, even for one minute or one hour, and live life under the assumption that God is alive and real and wants to pour out blessings on them. They can daydream about being abducted by space aliens, or what it would be like to win the Super Lotto, but they can't use their imaginations to dream what life would be like if Jesus Christ were their Lord and Savior. They can read books and watch movies about phony vampires and monsters, but not acknowledge the truth of Satan, fallen angels, and the implications of eternal life.

Truth Heals

When Jesus said Satan was the father of lies He didn't make a distinction between little lies and big lies. The difference between little lies and big lies is like the difference between white magic and black magic, which isn't a difference at all. No matter what the size, lies are an indication of the corruption inside the heart of the person who tells them. They can also corrupt the hearer of the lie, as in the case of the man of God who was killed by a lion. There is a difference between making a mistake and confessing it, and telling a lie and expecting someone else to believe it. When that happens the hearer becomes corrupted right along with the teller of the lie. We may not lie, but if we willingly go along with someone else's falsehood we are going to be infected by their spirit.

That is one reason God loved King David so much. David committed adultery and had Uriah the Hittite killed, but when confronted by Nathan the prophet, David didn't lie or make any excuses (2 Sam. 12). David probably wasn't alone when Nathan confronted him. He was probably surrounded by members of his court and servants. He was a very powerful king and could have had Nathan killed for speaking as he did. That is how many kings did business back then and some still do it today. Nathan laid the wood to the mighty king of Israel like a Marine drill sergeant would dress down a buck recruit in boot camp, and David didn't lift a finger in protest.

What did David do? He confessed. "I have sinned against the LORD" (2 Sam. 12:13). From what we know of David, this was no contrived confession of convenience to fool everyone about how sorry he was. David agreed with God's opinion of what he had done. David knew he was wrong and God was right and there was no room in between for any excuses or lying. There was no part of King David's heart and soul that did not genuinely grieve for the sin he had committed against his God whom he loved so much. And that is why he was "a man after [God's] own heart" (1 Sam. 13:14).

King David made some egregious mistakes in his life, but haven't we all? A man who was after God's own heart certainly could not have been a liar. King David joined the ranks of other great saints like Abraham, who was a "friend of God" (James 2:23), and Daniel, who was "greatly beloved" (Dan. 10:19), and Job, who was "a perfect and an upright man" (Job 1:8). Praise God that through the righteousness of Jesus Christ we too might aspire to join the ranks of great God-fearing men such as David, Abraham, Daniel, and Job.

No Such Thing As Bad Luck

"Let no corrupt communication proceed out of your mouth, but that which is good to the use of edifying, that it may minister grace unto the hearers. And grieve not the holy Spirit of God, whereby ye are sealed unto the day of redemption" (Eph. 4:29–30). Lying is one of the quickest ways to quench the Holy Spirit. Paul says in Romans 1:18, "The wrath of God is revealed from heaven against all ungodliness and unrighteousness of men, who hold the truth in unrighteousness." He goes on to say those who "changed the truth of God into a lie" were turned over "unto vile affections" (Rom. 1:25–26).

We all slip up and make mistakes like lying. If we repent and confess our sin, God will forgive us. In fact, He blots out our transgressions for His own sake "and will not remember" our sins (Isa. 43:25). Lying without remorse or regret, however, is an entirely different matter. Eventually it will become a part of the fabric of a person's character and personality. It has been my experience that people like that often become mean and ornery as they get older, sometimes downright strange. They have a difficult time separating fact from fiction about themselves, and they are deeply troubled and fearful in their souls and have no idea why. If truth were a candle, in some people, it is barely flickering, and in others it has gone out completely.

First Kings 22 tells the end of a man whose candle had burned out in what might be one of the earliest pieces of writing using the literary genre of satire. In this chapter, wicked King Ahab of Israel has already decided to go to Ramoth-gilead to do battle, and he wants good King Jehoshaphat of Judah to come along. So Ahab gathers about 400 prophets together and asks them if he should do battle or not. The prophets knew what answer the king wanted to hear, so they lied and told Ahab the Lord would be with him in battle. Jehoshaphat saw right away the fix he was in, so he made Ahab inquire of a real prophet.

So Micaiah the prophet shows up, and Ahab's messenger has already told him what the right answer was. Micaiah didn't seem to show any respect for the king, and said to Ahab, "Go, and prosper" (v. 15). There was something about Micaiah's demeanor that even wicked old Ahab could see through, and he knew the prophet was pulling his leg. Ahab made Micaiah tell the truth, so the prophet gave a true prophecy, but he may have added a little embellishment of his own.

If we are to believe Micaiah's prophecy literally, God was sitting on His throne with all the host of heaven standing around Him. He was probably stroking His chin, thinking aloud, wondering how He was going to get rid of that wicked Ahab. Some of the angels and spirits offered up suggestions and ideas, brainstorming on how to help God solve the problem. None of the ideas were any good until one spirit came up and said, "I will persuade him. And the LORD said unto him, Wherewith? And he said, I will go forth, and I will be a lying spirit in the mouth of all his prophets. And he said, Thou shalt persuade him, and prevail also: go forth, and do so" (v. 21–22).

Now this probably isn't how it really happened, but Ahab knew Micaiah was a true prophet of God (v. 8). Micaiah told Ahab he wouldn't return alive from Ramoth-gilead, but the king wasn't interested in hearing the truth because his mind was already made up. He had his will set that he was going to Ramoth-gilead and it didn't matter what anyone said. Here is a case of a man exercising his will to override what he knew to be true, in order to believe a lie that led to his death. "And a certain man drew a bow at a venture, and smote the king of Israel between the joints of the harness" (v. 34). That was no lucky shot but neither was it the king's bad luck. That arrow had "Ahab" written all over it and hit the bull's-eye because he was a wicked man.

Some people become so willfully disobedient and stubborn they absolutely refuse to recognize truth. They keep grasping at lies until that is the only thing left to hold onto. Logic, reason, and evidence become irrelevant until, like Ahab, the only thing that will prevail is a lie. They may also become indignant when confronted with the truth, as Ahab did when he had Micaiah placed in prison before he went to battle. No one likes to be confronted with the fact that they have lied, like the prophet Nathan did to King David. The best way to guard against that is not to do anything we might be tempted to lie about. There is an old saying: "Character is what we do when no one is watching." Let's rephrase this in the context of the fear of God: "Character is what we do when only God is watching." If we do make a mistake like lying, the sooner we confess and put it behind us the better off we will be. Otherwise, we will always be casting fretful glances over our shoulder waiting for it to catch up with us.

Esteeming the Truth

Proverbs 12:22 tells us what God thinks when He hears people lie. "Lying lips are abomination to the LORD." As Christians, we should agree with God. When we hear people tell lies and it makes us angry, there is nothing wrong with that. God gets angry as well. We need not apologize when lies make us angry. In fact, if lies don't make a person angry it is probable that person is unrighteous and ungodly. Those are harsh words, but those are the apostle Paul's words in Romans 1:18, noted previously.

The damage lies cause can be worse than broken bones and torn flesh. At least the flesh can heal, but lies can cause irreparable damage. God can forgive and even forget our sins, as noted in Isaiah 43:25. People can forgive another's sins, but it is very hard for us to forget. Lies are like deep cuts; they may heal, but they leave behind an ugly scar.

As Christians, it is vital we hold fast to the truth in all things. When Christians lie it is a signal to unbelievers there is no difference between them and us. Faith in Jesus Christ and our fear of God wasn't strong enough to keep us from lying, so what good must it be? As Christians, we are different from unbelievers, separated to God because of our uncompromising fidelity to truth. Pontius Pilate feared man more than God and couldn't recognize truth when it was standing before him in the person of Jesus Christ. King Ahab didn't fear God, wouldn't listen to truth from the prophet Micaiah, and lost his life as a result. If Christians allow the truth to be compromised, we will let go of our fear of God, and soon the ability to discern truth will be lost as well.

We should always rest on the Word of God to make sure we are in position to boldly, and in the spirit of truth, denounce those who use lies to undermine the Bible and our faith. We should be fearful lest we become mean-spirited, condescending, intolerant, prideful, or even rude. Those are the tools of our adversaries, and they use them with more effectiveness than any Christian ever could. We should avoid competing with unbelievers to see who is the most mean and spiteful, but if it becomes a contest we should gracefully step aside and let them win. We must "be strong and of a good courage" (Josh. 1:6) if we are to take hold of God's promise for our lives. Jesus Christ is also the Lion of the tribe of Judah, and through His courage, we can face down any fears that might cause us to shortchange the truth and fall short of His blessings.

CHAPTER 12

LONGSUFFERING MEANS SUFFERING FOR A REALLY LONG TIME

The Lord is not slack concerning his promise, as some men count slackness; but is longsuffering to us-ward, not willing that any should perish, but that all should come to repentance.

—2 PETER 3:9

MANY CHRISTIANS, AND unbelievers as a rule, make the unfortunate determination that the Bible is not worth their time to read, much less study. It may be a good book but they are too busy with other things, and reading it anytime in the near future isn't on their agenda. Many profess to be Christians, and they may even get teary-eyed when they see a movie where Jesus suffers on the cross. But acknowledging the Bible as the inerrant, inspired Word of God is a step many won't take. Admitting the Bible is what it claims to be would carry with it the responsibility to understand and know its contents. The right of man to define truth would have to be forfeited and ceded to God. This would necessitate changes in lifestyle and, rather than being inconvenienced, many choose ignorance.

Willfully choosing ignorance is the same as being disobedient and rebellious. God "is longsuffering to us-ward, not willing that any should perish, but that all come to repentance" (2 Pet. 3:9). Stated another way, God has been suffering for an extremely long time, at least since Adam and Eve ate the forbidden fruit of the tree of the knowledge of good and evil (Gen. 3:6). We know God can suffer as evidenced by Jesus' horrible and painful death on the cross. When we fail to acknowledge His suffering we are no better than a common thief or murderer who is ambivalent to the suffering of his victim and disinterested in his plight. It is easy to commit a crime against someone we don't know and can't see, while remaining blissfully ignorant of the consequences. If we had to look directly into the eyes of those we victimize and experience the same pain we were about to inflict, it would be much harder to commit the crime. God continues to graciously suffer victimization against His holiness by mankind in order that we not perish, and endures anguish that we should come to repentance.

When we sin against God, we victimize Him. We may not look into His eyes, but He is looking directly into ours. Whether we admit it or not, a sin against another person is a sin against Jesus Christ, because we renew His pain and suffering as a creation gone astray. Putting a human face on this discussion, how many parents enjoy seeing their child tormented by a bully, or abused by a pedophile, or commit a crime and be sent to jail? No one enjoys watching those they love and are closest to suffer or inflict pain on others. Because we were created in "his own image" (Gen. 1:27), the same things that cause us suffering cause God to suffer. If we hate seeing those we love suffer or commit crimes, why would we think God is ambivalent or disinterested?

We may think some crimes are victimless if they only cause damage to ourselves, like chronic gambling or alcoholism. How many children enjoy having a father who is a drunk, or vice versa? Although we don't see His suffering or hear His cries of pain, we victimize Jesus when we sin against Him. Victims don't usually sit in judgment of those who have harmed them, but it is well to remember when we sin against Jesus we will also be judged by Him. There is no such thing as a victimless crime. Taken in this context, the fear of God seems rather sensible.

"Behold, I send you forth as sheep in the midst of wolves: be ye therefore wise as serpents, and harmless as doves" (Matt. 10:16). Standing tall as a Christian is not for the faint of heart. There are many who neither fear nor love God that will work feverishly to destroy our faith. There is a clear line of demarcation between truth and falsity, good and evil, and right and wrong. Christians must resist the efforts of those with no fear of God to erase, blur, or shift that line, and in the process define for us which side we stand on. We must be certain in our spirit exactly where that line is, and then we must decide where we will stand. God is longsuffering and He gives us plenty of time to determine where the line between good and evil is drawn. His patience is inexhaustible, but if we incessantly pretend that no such line exists we will eventually run the clock out of time.

Ambivalence and uncertainty toward the things of God is like a screw in a piece of machinery that vibrates loose until it finally falls out. It may take months or even years, but eventually the machinery reaches the right resonant frequency, the screw works loose and falls out, and we were never aware it was happening. Ambivalence only encourages further efforts by the wolves to shake our faith, and the foundation slowly erodes and develops cracks until everything collapses. Christians don't allow the fears of the world to displace our fear of God, nor do we have anything to fear from the wolf pack. The fear of God distinguishes us.

REDEMPTION VALUE: ZERO

When the fear of God is completely absent from an individual or a society, judgment from the Lord can't be far behind. Jesus is our Redeemer but not everyone has a redemptive value. Out here in California, beverage bottles often have a redemption value stamped on their side. An empty bottle may be worth a nickel if you take it to a recycling center. It isn't worth a nickel to me, but if it is worth a nickel to someone else that means its value is a nickel. When we stand before Jesus Christ for judgment, He is going to look at us to see if we have any redemptive value. If we have faith in Christ, He will redeem us, and if we don't have faith in Christ He won't. It is as simple as that. If I take a bottle with a redemptive value of a nickel and break it to bits, take it down to the recycling center and ask for a nickel, the guy is going to tell me that bottle has no redemptive value. Now it isn't worth anything to anybody and is fit only to be thrown in the trash.

Later we will see that this is what happened to the Canaanite civilization. Jesus evaluated the Canaanites to be of no redemptive value whatsoever and passed judgment on them. They had erased the line between good and evil, assigned equal values to right and wrong, and elbowed God out of every aspect of their society. They committed crimes without regard to the victims and had become so evil that the spirit of God was completely absent in them. They severed their remaining connection to God, and once it was gone there was no way it could be reestablished. They were as useless as a burned-out lightbulb.

NAILING DOWN SPIRIT

We are redeemed through faith in Christ. Initially, God invested in each of us by imparting to us His Spirit and creating in us a living soul (Gen. 2:7). Perhaps it is impossible to discern where the Spirit of God starts and the spirit and soul of man ends. Do they overlap on the edges like shingles on a roof, or are they cross-tied like railroad tracks and run parallel? Does man's spirit join with God's to form a new compound like salt dissolving in water or are they linked together like a chain? Are they welded together in a strong, unbreakable bond or are they attached by fusible links that melt and separate when things get too hot?

Any hardware store is loaded with multitudinous fasteners for joining all kinds of different things together. There are staples, nails, rivets, hooks, nuts and bolts, brackets, glues, cements, mortars, adhesives, couplings, elbows, and just about any device a person could imagine for connecting almost anything to something else. God's Spirit and the spirit and soul of man don't fit into any of these fastener categories. Humanist philosophers, psychologists, and theologians have come up with terms and theories to try to capture the definition and essence of spirit, and they all fall short of the mark.

The human body also consists of a multitude of fasteners. If a person takes two heavy dumbbells and holds them at his side, eventually he will have to release them. They will cause strain on the legs, knees, wrists, elbows, shoulders, and hands. Eventually some muscle, ligament, tendon, or joint, whichever is weakest, is going to reach a point of stress failure and the dumbbells will have to be dropped. If this process is repeated at periodic intervals the person will eventually gain strength and be able to hold the dumbbells for longer lengths of time. But God's Spirit and man's spirit aren't fastened together like the human body.

Man's spirit isn't fastened to God's Spirit like a nail through a board, or like a finger connected to a hand. The Lord has more fasteners in His toolbox than any Home Depot, and He uses them all in different ways to connect His Spirit with ours. Each one is a little different and He is willing to do whatever it takes to get the job done. He will wrestle with us like He wrestled with Jacob (Gen. 32:24), He will wash our feet if He has to (John 13:5), and He will even pour His blood out on the ground.

GOD'S STRANGE WORK

The last thing God wants is to have one of us, to whom He has imparted His Spirit and whose soul He has created, stand before Him possessing a redemption value of zero. "He telleth the number of the stars; he calleth them all by their names" (Ps. 147:4). No two stars are the same, and the same is true of the people God has created. He knows us all and is interested in every aspect of our lives, as any loving parent would be. God isn't up in heaven making people and stars on a manufacturer's assembly line, like a Ford truck or a toaster oven. He said, "since the beginning of the world men have not heard, nor perceived by the ear, neither hath the eye seen, O God, beside thee, what he hath prepared for him that waiteth for him" (Isa. 64:4). "For, behold, I create new heavens and a new earth" (Isa. 65:17). God is the Great Creator, but He is also the

106

Great Artist. Everything He makes is original, and wonderful and distinct to the praise of His glory. It is grievous to Him to have a part of His creation lose all the value that He initially invested in it.

When people have relationships with each other, they share a common interest that connects them together. When a relationship is strained, it places stress on that connection, sometimes to the point where only a thin sliver of thread remains. At the end of a relationship, when that last thread is cut, it is unlikely the relationship can ever be mended. Jesus never cuts that thread, people do. When that last thread is cut there isn't anything left for the Lord to fasten onto and He has to let that person go. If we cut that last thread to Christ, we freely repudiate any redemptive value we might have once had.

THE THINNEST OF THREADS

So what does any of this have to do with slaying the fear in our lives and overcoming the challenges we face? If we don't fear God, the answer is nothing. If we do fear God, the answer is in the Spirit of the longsuffering God that resides in each of us. God has invested us with His Spirit so that we may overcome our fears and challenges. But we must have faith that God is who He says He is, and that as a loving parent He wants only the best for us. We must also remember the lesson of the twelve spies from Numbers 13 and 14. If we don't believe that the Spirit of God resides in us, and that we aren't able to conquer all our fears, He will agree with us. Whatever we choose to believe will become our reality.

As Henry Ford once said, "Whether you think you can or think you can't—you're right." We must have faith that the promises of God will work in our lives. If the promises don't work then our faith is of no value. We will be completely at the mercy of any dragons that chase us down, so we might as well surrender. Because God is longsuffering and merciful, He will give us time to grow in our faith. But in order for our faith to grow we must constantly look in His direction. If we spend a lifetime looking away from God, some day we will lose all chances of ever making a connection with His Spirit. When the investment God has made in us of His Spirit is lost, our redemptive value will be lost as well.

CHAPTER 13

THE DESTRUCTION OF A CIVILIZATION

But of the cities of these people, which the LORD thy God doth give thee for an inheritance, thou shalt save alive nothing that breatheth.

—DEUTERONOMY 20:16

SINCE THE SUBJECT of the Canaanites was discussed in the last chapter, this seems an opportune point to examine what they did that caused God to give them up for lost. This is important for us to understand because if we are to have mastery over our fears we can't repeat the mistakes of the Canaanites. We are given their example in the Bible so we may avoid their fate, and we should not presumptuously assume the evils they committed have no relevance to modern society.

The Canaanites did eventually learn what it meant to fear God, but it was the type of dreadful fear that must come to a criminal when sentence is passed and a hooded executioner stands ready to perform his task. The inhabitants of Canaan were so far removed from the things of God they possessed no redemptive value. Their society had become so diseased and corrupt that, absent any potential for repentance, only God's judgment could end their reprobate behavior.

The Book of Joshua documents the destruction of the Canaanites. It was Joshua's task to lead the people and take the land as God had commanded: "Every place that the sole of your foot shall tread upon, that have I given unto you, as I said unto Moses" (Josh. 1:3). There was no promise made to Joshua that his assignment would be easy. Three times in the first chapter God told him to "be strong and of a good courage." Then the people of Israel told Joshua they would follow his commands, but they wanted him to "be strong and of a good courage." Joshua was told a total of four times in the first chapter to be "strong and of a good courage," and God offered other words of encouragement assuring him of success. As the leader of the people and with God as Commander in Chief, Joshua could not afford to show fear or trepidation about the task he had been assigned.

God explains that task in Deuteronomy 20. In verses 10 through 15 God provides detailed guidance to Israel regarding how to handle the people in cities that were very far away. An offer of peace would be made, which, if accepted, would result in all the people becoming servants to the nation of Israel. If the peace were not accepted all the males would be killed, and the women and children would be taken by Israel along with the property as spoil. Presumably over time the women and children would be integrated into the nation of Israel.

Deuteronomy 20:16–17, however, gave the children of Israel a distinctly different charge for handling a specifically named and particularly reprobate group of people much closer to home. This was a charge to commit genocide. Every living thing that breathed—every man, woman, child, and all the animals among these groups—were to be utterly destroyed by Joshua's army at the commandment of God. About the only thing to be left alive were the trees (Deut. 10:19). God did not want any remaining element of those corrupt and infectious societies to pollute the children of Israel. It would not have been possible for Israel to remain consecrated to God if any aspect of the vile and debased Canaanite civilization were integrated into the inheritance of even one of the twelve tribes.

This commandment originated in Genesis 15. Abraham, after fighting off fowls that were trying to eat the carcasses of his sacrifice to God, fell into a deep sleep. A great darkness came upon him, and God told him his seed, the people of Israel, would be afflicted for 400 years (in Egypt as it turns out). "But in the fourth generation they [the children of Israel] shall come hither again: for the iniquity of the Amorites is not yet full" (Gen. 15:16).

> Thus saith the LORD the King of Israel, and his redeemer the LORD of hosts; I am the first, and I am the last; and beside me there is no God.
> —ISAIAH 44:6

God knew the Amorites and the other people of Canaan were evil during the time of Abraham. And because He knows the beginning and the end, God knew they would be even worse after 400 years. But in the interim, God sent Jacob and his sons to Egypt under the protection of Joseph, and the children of Israel multiplied and remained separate as God had intended. Eventually they came under bondage to the Egyptians, but it was God's plan all along that Israel "be a peculiar treasure unto me above all people: for all the earth is mine: And ye shall be unto me a kingdom of priests, and an holy nation" (Exod. 19:5–6). When Jacob and his sons left Canaan to go to Egypt, however, they didn't pack God up in a suitcase and just bring Him along. God is all-present, all-powerful, and all-knowing. He was already in Egypt when Jacob got there, but He also never left Canaan.

The Bible doesn't always give us every bit of information we would like to have, but it does tell us what we need to know. Starting at Genesis 11:10, the focus of the Bible shifts to follow the line of Shem, one of Noah's sons. From this point on, the Word of God is primarily addressing the line of Shem, through to Abraham and down to King David, right on through to Jesus Christ the Messiah. Of course, Jesus has been called the "scarlet thread" that runs throughout the Bible from start to finish.

But just because the primary focus is on the line of Shem down to Jesus doesn't mean God was ignoring everybody else on the face of the earth. He wasn't. God was and is involved in every aspect of every life of every person in every nation that ever has been, is, or will be. He was in the land of Canaan working with those people during the 400-year period when the iniquity of the Amorites was bad and getting worse. We know God was working with those people because the Bible tells us so.

In Genesis 14:18 we meet up with Melchizedek the king of Salem. "He was the priest of the most high God," and he brought Abraham some bread and wine. Some say Melchizedek was really Shem, the son of Noah. Others say he was really the pre-incarnate Jesus Christ, while still others say he was just a man. Whoever he was, one thing is certain: he was somebody special, and he knew and feared God. One other thing is certain: Salem later became known as Jerusalem, which indicates that particular spot on planet earth had some significance to God even before the children of Israel entered the Promised Land. It would be nice to know more about this story, but other than some passages in the Book of Hebrews, this is pretty much all we are given about Melchizedek.

In Genesis 20:2, Abraham tells a half-lie about his wife, Sarah, being his sister. So the king of Gerar, Abimelech, took Sarah into his house, probably to be a concubine. God told Abimelech, "Behold, thou art but a dead man" (v. 3), because Sarah was set aside as part of the line that would produce the Messiah, and this Philistine king didn't fit in. Abimelech was operating out of ignorance and pleaded to God for his life. In verse 6, God tells him, "I know that thou didst this in the integrity of thy heart." Abimelech gave Sarah back to Abraham, chastised the two of them, and God healed Abimelech and his family. In Genesis 26, Isaac pulls the same stunt Abraham had pulled, with his wife, Rebekah. He also does it in Gerar and to a king named Abimelech, and the results were much the same as before. Later in Genesis 26:28, Abimelech made a covenant with Isaac, because he knew "the LORD was with" him. We can be certain the Philistine Abimelech was a man who feared God.

In Numbers 22 we are introduced to Balaam the son of Beor, and he is a square peg in a round hole. Balak, the king of Moab, wanted Balaam to curse the children of Israel, but God told Balaam he had better not. Instead, Balaam advised Balak to use the women of Moab to seduce and corrupt the men of Israel, and that worked. To get the girls, the men of Israel bowed down to the Moabite gods, the Lord's anger was kindled, and 24,000 Israelites died of a plague as a result. But again, one thing was certain: whoever this Balaam was, he knew who the living God was. In fact, from Numbers 22–24, God and Balaam were having quite a conversation. Apparently Balaam must have missed some of the finer points God was trying to make because the Israelites "slew [him] with the sword" in Numbers 31:8.

We know from Genesis 21:18 that God was going to make Ishmael, Abraham's son through Hagar, a great nation. Ishmael did become a great nation, and it is safe to say this son of Abraham knew God. Over 400 years later, Jethro, a Midianite and Moses' father-in-law, knew who the Lord was and "that the LORD is greater than all gods" (Exod. 18:11). By this time, word had spread about God's wonders in Egypt, and there was no uncertainty down there about who God was.

Even after Israel had finished wandering in the wilderness the people of Jericho knew who the Lord was. In Joshua 2:10–11 Rahab the harlot said they had heard about how the Lord had dried up the Red Sea forty years earlier, and "our hearts did melt, neither did there remain any more courage in any man, because of you: for the LORD your God, he is God in heaven above, and in earth beneath." Those people in Jericho knew who God was and they feared Him, but the only one who had any saving faith was Rahab, the same Rahab (Rachab) mentioned in the genealogy of Jesus Christ in Matthew 1:5.

The point of these examples is that the people in Canaan had every opportunity to turn in worship to the living God, but they just didn't want to. While the children of Israel were in bondage in Egypt, God was working with those people to turn them in repentance but they wouldn't listen. The Bible doesn't give a lot of detail about what went on during that period of time, but because God's mercy outweighs His justice, He gave them over 400 years to turn from their evil ways. The people in Jericho could have turned to God but they refused, so the walls fell down and only Rahab was spared.

God is as holy and righteous today as He was then, and

He makes no secret of the fact that a day of judgment and reckoning comes upon every man. The clock may run out on our lives of flesh before the Lord's Second Coming, or it may not. But "every knee shall bow, every tongue shall swear" (Isa. 45:23) that Jesus Christ is Lord. "For we shall all stand before the judgment seat of Christ" (Rom. 14:10).

The Lord is merciful, but no one can say how late is too late for salvation. It wasn't too late for Rahab and her family, but time ran out on the rest of the folks in Jericho. They could see the army of Israel from the city walls, marching around for seven days with the ark of the covenant, and they stayed shut up inside. Those people inside the walls of Jericho were probably bending the knee to Baal, praying to him to save them, but they wouldn't bend their knees to the only One who could do them any good. They could have turned to the living God at the last moment, but instead they severed any connection they had to Him that remained.

WELCOME TO THE JUNGLE

> Not for thy righteousness, or for the uprightness of thine heart, dost thou go to possess their land: but for the wickedness of these nations the LORD thy God doth drive them out from before thee, and that he may perform the word which the LORD sware unto thy fathers, Abraham, Isaac, and Jacob. Understand, therefore, that the LORD thy God giveth thee not this good land to possess it for thy righteousness; for thou art a stiffnecked people.
>
> —DEUTERONOMY 9:5–6

Here God makes it clear why Israel is getting the land. It isn't some special merit the people of Israel possess. Earlier we discussed the Jewish tradition that God's mercy and grace exceed His requirement for justice and

115

punishment by at least five-hundred-fold. A balance is sometimes used to symbolize justice (Dan. 5:27). If you put 500 pounds on the mercy side of the balance, and one pound on the judgment side, that balance would hit rock bottom on the mercy side. But if you added one pound a year on the judgment side, and you never took anything off, after 500 years that balance is going to start tilting the other way. And after 501 years it is going to hit rock bottom on the judgment side, and that's exactly where the Canaanites were.

Deuteronomy 18:10–12 lays out the case against the Canaanites. God tells the children of Israel exactly why He is driving out the Canaanites and warns them not to repeat their mistakes. It is relevant today why God's balance of justice tipped from mercy to judgment. "Jesus Christ the same yesterday, and to day, and for ever" (Heb. 13:8). God hasn't changed, and sadly, if mankind has changed, it is probably for the worse.

> There shall not be found among you any one that maketh his son or his daughter to pass through the fire, or that useth divination, or an observer of times, or an enchanter, or a witch, Or a charmer, or a consulter with familiar spirits, or a wizard, or a necromancer. For all that do these things are an abomination unto the LORD: and because of these abominations the LORD thy God doth drive them out from before thee.
> —DEUTERONOMY 18:10–12

An abomination is something that is disgusting, vile, and abhorrent. Proverbs 20:27 states, "The spirit of man is the candle of the LORD, searching all the inward parts of the belly." In Proverbs 24:20 we read, "For there shall be no reward to the evil man; the candle of the wicked shall be put out." God knew what those Canaanites had been up to, because the spirit inside of them belonged to Him. God's candle isn't like a barely flickering flame, casting long, dark, gloomy shadows that shudder in the breeze. His candle is bright, and there aren't any shadows or corners He can't see into. The same thing that was true of the Canaanites is true of us today. The Lord's candle searches all the inward parts of a person, and if there's something disgusting, vile, and abhorrent inside of us, He sees it.

The Canaanites were driven from the land because they were heavily involved in idolatry, the supernatural, and occult activities. They were more interested in worshiping the things of Satan than the things of God. The Lord looked into the innermost part of the Canaanites' souls, and there was nothing there for His Spirit to latch on to and redeem. They had cut the last connecting thread they had to God and were totally committed to Satan. Activities similar to those of the Canaanites are present today in the United States and around the world to various degrees. Let's examine these activities and try to determine what it is about them that God hates, and how they corrupt people.

Sacrifice of children to the false god Molech would involve burning the child in the arms of the idol and the drinking of human blood. Leviticus 17:11 reads, "For the life of the flesh is in the blood: and I have given it to you upon the altar to make an atonement for your souls: for it is the blood that maketh an atonement for the soul." This was true under the old dispensation of law and it is true today under the dispensation of grace. Under the sacrificial system, God always designated one spot, either the tabernacle or the temple, where animal sacrifices were to take place, never human. Under no circumstances were the Israelites allowed to drink blood of any kind.

"And almost all things are by the law purged with blood; and without shedding of blood is no remission" (Heb. 9:22). The remission of sin today is by the shed blood of Jesus Christ, who is the Mediator between God and men. "For this purpose the Son of God was manifested, that he might destroy the works of the devil" (1 John 3:8). The devil's work set in motion the curse of Genesis 2:17, when God told Adam "thou shalt surely die" if he ate the forbidden fruit. Jesus shed His blood to undo the curse that is the work of Satan. Human sacrifice and the drinking of blood is a direct repudiation of Jesus Christ and represents a wholehearted embrace of Satan and death. These are not the actions of one who fears God and loves Him with all their heart, mind, and soul.

Human sacrifice, or any other kind of ceremonial occult sacrifice, sends a very clear and direct message to God Almighty. It is a repudiation of everything the Lord Jesus Christ has done for us. It is a rejection of His creation, His shed blood, the cross, His plan of salvation, and His grace and mercy. It is a rejection of the sovereignty of God the Creator in an attempt to replace it with our own.

THINGS GET WORSE HERE EVERY DAY

In Ecclesiastes 7:10, King Solomon cautions, "Say not thou, What is the cause that the former days were better than these? for thou dost not enquire wisely concerning this." We could rephrase this as, "Say not thou, What is the cause that the former days are worse than these?" and be on safe ground. How bad was Canaan compared to today? Only God knows, and He's keeping His opinion to Himself for now. The fact that the God of Creation and His divine sovereignty is being ignored and rejected today, however, is not a recent development.

118

> The secret things belong unto the LORD our God: but
> those things which are revealed belong unto us and to
> our children for ever, that we may do all the words of
> this law.
>
> —DEUTERONOMY 29:29

Moses wrote these words at the direction of God. What did he mean when he referred to the "secret things" that belong to God? This is Moses' farewell address to the twelve tribes before he died, and in context, he was warning them not to go and follow after gods other than the God of Israel. The supernatural and occult activities of Deuteronomy 18:10–12 describes some of the general practices the Canaanites followed to worship their false gods, who were in fact demons, or fallen angels.

God has placed these "secret things" of the supernatural and the occult off limits. Nevertheless, the Canaanites ignored God's sovereign right to place certain things out of bounds, and people today continue to do the same. Forbidden practices that people commonly engage in today include horoscopes and astrology, tarot cards and palm reading, séances, witchcraft, hypnotism, spiritualism, and other activities that fall in the category of occult. God-fearing Christians should never engage in these types of activities.

God hasn't fully explained why all these things are off limits. If He explained everything there wouldn't be any "secret things" left, and in His divine sovereignty He has reserved these for Himself and, presumably, His angels. The Lord has drawn a line in the sand between our temporal world and the world of angels, or the occult, and He didn't ask for anyone's permission before doing so. One thing we can be certain of is He did it for our own good. He didn't do it because He is mean or because He is greedy and wants to withhold all the good things for Himself, or because He wants us to fall short of enjoying all His love and grace. He placed those things out of bounds for our benefit, even though we might not understand all the reasons. When Christians get involved in anything having to do with the occult, no matter how harmless it seems, we are opening the door to spirits in our life that we want nothing to do with. Christians should treat activities such as palm reading, horoscopes, psychic hotlines, mediums, hypnosis, séances, witchcraft, and any other borderline occult activity like a communicable disease.

In fact, we should be very careful about the objects we have in our house. This isn't superstitious; it is just common sense and obedience to God. That woman I mentioned a couple of chapters ago, the one who prays to a shrine of Judas, gave my wife a teddy bear. She said the bear had a curse on it and had brought her nothing but bad luck, so she gave it to my wife. I used the bear for a three-point shot at the trash can, missed, but got the follow-up slam-dunk. Why would we want that in our house? This isn't a dissertation on demons, but we should not have objects of pagan worship in our house or anything that might carry a curse. We shouldn't have any dragon or demon statues, paintings or games, no prayer wheels, no books on magic or horoscopes, no tarot cards, no cute little charms we picked up on vacation in the Caribbean, or any item that we are aware of that speaks to the occult. And just to make a clean sweep of the house, any dirty books or magazines ought to go in the trash as well.

If your three-year-old nephew, Johnny, found a bright, shiny, nuclear radioactive isotope, would you let him play with it? Would you let him roll it around in his mouth to see what it tasted like, or stick it in his eye to find out if he could see through it? Would you let him sleep with it under his pillow as a charm for good luck? Why would God allow us to tamper with things that have a supernatural nature or are of the occult that we don't understand, can't control, and will harm us? God wants to protect us because He loves us and doesn't want to see us placed in bondage by some occult force that could turn into a spiritual Chernobyl.

YOU LEARN TO LIVE LIKE AN ANIMAL

Leviticus 20 also gives a detailed list of prohibited activities the Canaanites engaged in. In addition to occult activities and human sacrifice, various forms of illicit sex, including incest, homosexuality, and bestiality were prevalent. God warned the Israelites, "Ye shall not walk in the manners of the nation, which I cast out before you: for they committed all these things, and therefore I abhorred them" (Lev. 20:23).

Before anyone gets too sickened reading about the Canaanites, we will take the subject in a different direction. The Canaanites provide a useful illustration of behaviors Christians must not engage in if we are to avoid the spirit of fear. The Canaanites had a dreadful and terrifying fear of the holy, just, and righteous God which, as it turns out, was wholly warranted. Just as the thief on the cross in Luke 23:42 turned to Christ and was saved, the Canaanites could have turned to God in repentance at the last possible moment, but they just didn't want to.

Some may argue that we are not nearly as bad as the Canaanites because after all no one in any civilized nation of the world condones human sacrifice and the drinking of their blood. For those in this country and elsewhere, however, who worship at the altar of aborted human fetuses, it is a difference with fine distinction.

Christians today have no need to feel the type of dreadful fear the Canaanites experienced. If a Christian does have that dreadful fear, there is something terribly wrong that needs to be fixed pronto. My guess would be, in a case like that, the Christian knows exactly what the problem is and how to fix it, and he is probably the only one who knows why he hasn't fixed it. Even in that situation, there is still time to get down on our knees, sort things out, fess up to the truth, and get right with God.

"What is this then that is written, The stone which the builders rejected, the same is become the head of the corner? Whosoever shall fall upon that stone shall be broken; but on whomsoever it shall fall, it will grind him to powder" (Luke 20:17–18). Any Christian who has ever been broken before the Lord knows exactly what these verses mean, and I certainly understand them. Any Christian who has a dreadful fear of God is overdue to "fall upon that stone" which is Jesus Christ. We will be broken, but the Lord will lift us up on our feet, put His hand on our shoulder, call us friend, and get us back on the right track. Unless we turn our backs to God, we need not fear suffering the same fate as the Canaanites.

CHAPTER 14

FIRE FROM THE LORD

I will be sanctified in them that come nigh me,
and before all the people I will be glorified.

—LEVITICUS 10:3

THE HOLINESS OF God may be understood as one of
His personal attributes, just as lovingkindness, longsuffering, grace, and mercy are attributes. We fear a
God who is holy, that is, He is a spiritually pure and sinless
being. When we sanctify God, we recognize His sinless perfection, and explicitly acknowledge that we fall short of His
immeasurable glory. The holy and righteous God is someone to be reverenced and respected, and under no circumstances is He to be trifled with.

In the Old Testament the Mosaic Law was given by God
to Moses, who acted as an intermediary. Moses feared
God, so when God spoke to him Moses gave Him his
undivided attention. There was never a time when Moses

was too busy with duties more pressing than listening to God. Just like a human parent with a child, when the parent is giving instruction they appreciate it when the child listens. When the parent gives very specific and detailed instructions for the child's benefit and welfare, and the child becomes insolent and disrespectful, the parent is going to become righteously angry.

God has laid out a formal plan of salvation and presented it to fallen mankind through His written word. "Jesus saith unto him, I am the way, the truth, and the life: no man cometh unto the Father, but by me" (John 14:6). In this age of grace we are saved by faith through Jesus Christ, "for there is none other name under heaven given among men, whereby we must be saved" (Acts 4:12). God has made no secret of the path to eternal salvation and, like any parent, He expects us to pay attention and take Him seriously. If we don't, then like an insolent child who is disrespectful to their parent, dreadful fear of punishment is merited.

THE UNBEATEN PATH TO THE HOLY OF HOLIES

The Father is in the heavenly holy of holies, which was represented first by the tabernacle and later by the temple. The high priest was allowed to enter the holy of holies once a year on the Day of Atonement. Today Jesus Christ is our High Priest: "By his own blood he entered in once into the holy place, having obtained eternal redemption for us" (Heb. 9:12). Jesus is in "heaven itself, now to appear in the presence of God for us" (Heb. 9:24). Scripture tells us there's only one entrance into the holy of holies. No side or rear entrances are mentioned. The path to the earthly holy of holies wasn't well-beaten because the high priest only entered once per year.

There are some pretty tough patches of ground at the end of the Book of Exodus and through Leviticus, but God provides very precise information in these sections that is worth careful examination. Exodus 30 discusses the altar of incense before the curtain covering the entrance to the holy of holies. Moses was given an exact formula for the incense to be burned on the altar and it wasn't to be duplicated for any other purpose, at the risk of being cut off from the people. Verse 9 specifically states, "Ye shall offer no strange incense thereon." The priests were to keep this incense burning perpetually.

Earlier, in Exodus 28:34–35, we read Aaron was to wear a robe, and upon it were bells "upon the hem of the robe round about. And it shall be upon Aaron to minister: and his sound shall be heard when he goeth in unto the holy place before the LORD, and when he cometh out, that he die not." Certainly, God didn't require bells on the high priest's robe because he was afraid Aaron was going to sneak up on Him. God doesn't say why He wants Aaron to wear bells, but He makes it perfectly clear what will happen if he doesn't. He will die. Sometimes it would be nice to know why we are supposed to do certain things, but often we should just follow orders. If God says to wear bells, we should wear bells and not waste time arguing about it.

Before approaching God, Aaron and his sons are told how to dress, how and where to wash themselves, what to bring with them, how to sprinkle the blood, and a host of other specific details. Obviously God is very particular about how someone approaches His holy place, His holy of holies, and Him. He tells us these things not because He is mean and ornery, but for our own good. The method of how we approach God is different today than it was in the time of Moses and Aaron, but the guidance is no less clear.

It is critical when we approach God that we follow His rules and not buy into any of Satan's decoys and tricks.

"The LORD said unto my Lord, Sit thou on my right hand, Till I make thine enemies thy footstool" (Luke 20:42–43). Jesus Christ is presently sitting at God's right hand in the holy of holies. He paid the price of admission with blood.

In John 10, Jesus contrasts His mission with that of a thief sneaking his way into the sheepfold. The thief jumps over the fence and avoids the door at the front of the fold because that is where the shepherd is. "I am the door: by me if any man enter in, he shall be saved" (John 10:9). There is only one entrance to the holy of holies and that is Jesus Christ.

Paul tells us in Ephesians 2:18 that through Jesus "we both have access by one Spirit unto the Father." He states further, "For there is one God, and one mediator between God and men, the man Christ Jesus" (1 Tim. 2:5). And in Hebrews 7:25 it is written that Jesus "is able also to save them to the uttermost that come unto God by him, seeing he ever liveth to make intercession for them."

We have spent time talking about how to approach God in order to emphasize how important obedience is. Some cults would have us believe we can walk up to the holy of holies and knock on the door, peek our heads in, see God sitting there with His feet on His desk and ask Him if He could spare a few minutes. Leviticus 10, where two of Aaron's sons die, tells us otherwise. This is one section of the Word of God that Muslims, Jehovah's Witnesses, and a lot of other cults should take time studying. Showing deference, obedience, and fear to a holy God is not demeaning servitude, but rather sound judgment and wisdom.

STRANGE FIRE

Leviticus 10 describes a very hard lesson Aaron, his sons, and the children of Israel received. The lesson was learned at their expense and provided for our benefit.

> And Nadab and Abihu, the sons of Aaron, took either of them his censer, and put fire therein, and put incense thereon, and offered strange fire before the LORD, which he commanded them not. And there went out fire from the LORD, and devoured them, and they died before the LORD.
> —LEVITICUS 10:1–2

In verse 9 of this chapter, God gives Aaron a warning that seems to come from nowhere, about not drinking wine or strong drink when entering the tabernacle. The general consensus among commentators is that Nadab and Abihu were probably drunk when they offered the strange fire that caused their death. Now Moses was Aaron's younger brother, and he told two of his cousins to wrap the charred remains of Nadab and Abihu and take them out of the camp. Moses wrote the first five books of the Bible, and he may have been understating the case when describing the reaction of his brother, Aaron, to the death of two of his sons. In verse 3, we learn that after seeing his two sons die "Aaron held his peace."

Hollywood is able to produce very impressive special effects for the movie industry, but most of us have realized, especially since 9/11, that reality can be far more shocking and horrifying than a movie. What Aaron, Moses, and the children of Israel saw as Nadab and Abihu died must have remained indelibly etched in their memories. They had failed to glorify and sanctify God in the manner explained to them, and approached the Lord in a disrespectful and impudent way. The consequences must have been devastating to Aaron as he observed the burnt, smoldering bodies of his sons being carried away from camp. Aaron held his peace, but God only knows what he was thinking.

We are not given all the details of this story. We don't know if Aaron could have stopped his two sons from offering strange fire and failed to do so, or whether Aaron had been drinking as well. We don't know what the other sons of Aaron were doing at the time. We also don't know the eternal status of the souls of Nadab and Abihu. We can hope that despite failing in this instance, they are now with the Lord. God is merciful and fortunately, one mistake doesn't necessarily mean eternal damnation. The Lord may have just decided that after this event, their work was finished and it was time to call Nadab and Abihu home. One thing is likely: one hundred years or one thousand years from now, unless the Lord's Second Coming dictates otherwise, no one will remember you or me. But Nadab and Abihu will still be offered as examples for how seriously God takes this question of how we're to approach Him. "Heaven and earth shall pass away: but my words shall not pass away" (Luke 21:33).

Only God knows the intent that was in the hearts of Nadab and Abihu, and only He knows the intent in our hearts. If our hearts are ambivalent and disinterested, or worse yet insolent and disrespectful toward God, then dreadful fear would be appropriate. If someone turns in repentance to the Lord as the result of dreadful fear, that is not a bad thing. God does not choose to inflict dreadful fear upon us. But it can serve as a last, desperate, final chance to repent and grasp eternal life out of the jaws of death and the lake of fire.

Dreadful fear is the last line of defense against eternal damnation, however, it is unlikely anyone who has it is going to overcome any mountains in their life. Christians have no need to experience that kind of fear from a God whom we love with all our heart, mind, and soul. We should have strong confidence in Jesus Christ that those fears have no place in our life so that the mountains He sets before us can be overcome. As long as we are in Christ and aren't offering strange fire before the Lord we can rest easy that the path inside the holy of holies is wide open to us.

> Enter ye in at the strait gate: for wide is the gate, and broad is the way, that leadeth to destruction, and many there be which go in thereat: Because strait is the gate, and narrow is the way, which leadeth unto life, and few there be that find it.
>
> —MATTHEW 7:13–14

CHAPTER 15

THE FEAR
OF FALLING SHORT

Let us therefore fear, lest, a promise being
left us of entering into his rest, any of you
should seem to come short of it.

—HEBREWS 4:1

THERE IS A tremendous difference of opinion and
confusion among believers regarding the Holy
Spirit. The promise of the indwelling presence of
the Holy Spirit in born-again believers is a unique aspect
of the Christian faith. It represents God's extended hand to
fallen mankind to restore some of the fellowship lost in the
Garden of Eden. It doesn't necessarily mitigate or lessen the
consequences man faces because of his rebellion against
God. But it does offer the power of transformation and a
release from spiritual bondage that resulted from the curse
God pronounced in Genesis 3:15–19. It is through the Holy
Spirit that we learn the fear of God.

In some denominations there is significant emphasis

placed on baptism in the Holy Spirit, as well there should be. This is based on scripture such as Acts 2, which describes the Day of Pentecost after the resurrected Jesus Christ had ascended to heaven.

> And suddenly there came a sound from heaven as of a rushing mighty wind, and it filled all the house where they were sitting. And there appeared unto them cloven tongues like as of fire, and it sat upon each of them. And they were all filled with the Holy Ghost, and began to speak with other tongues, as the Spirit gave them utterance.
>
> —ACTS 2:2–4

FALSE COMPARISONS

Like everyone else, we have a tendency to compare ourselves with other Christians to see how we measure up. Is our Bible knowledge up to snuff like our Christian brothers or sisters? Why do the Smiths always seem to receive abundant blessings while the Joneses are always having trouble? And then there is the Holy Spirit baptism. Do I have it or not? The Smiths and Joneses say they have it, there are books written about it by people who have it, and all the preachers on TV say they have it. In fact, some folks give the impression that the Lord is sitting in heaven with His hand on the telephone, just waiting for it to ring so He can pick it up and answer their questions. Why am I the only one who seems to be coming up short?

If we could measure the indwelling presence of the Holy Spirit on a scale of 1 through 100, Jesus is the only One who has ever measured a perfect 100. In John 3:34, John the Baptist, in referring to Jesus, said, "For he whom God hath sent speaketh the words of God: for God giveth not the Spirit by measure unto him." The New International

Version translates that God gave Jesus "the Spirit without limit."

So with Jesus setting the standard with a perfect 100, presumably the rest of mankind falls somewhat below that. In 2 Kings 2:9, Elisha asked of Elijah, before Elijah was taken by God, that "a double portion of thy spirit be upon me." Elijah replied that if Elisha saw his translation to heaven it would be so. In verses 11 and 12 Elisha saw Elijah swept up by "a whirlwind into heaven," and subsequent events would indicate he did receive that double portion. Short of Jesus, and perhaps Moses, it is possible no other biblical character was filled with the Spirit of God to the extent Elisha was. It would be impossible for us, however, to accurately score him on our scale of 1 through 100. We could only assume it was a score less than 100, and if Elijah could be represented with the variable X, then Elisha would have 2X.

Born-again Christians have "the mind of Christ," (1 Cor. 2:16) that presumably comes through the Holy Spirit. As Jesus said, in referring to the Holy Spirit, "He shall glorify me: for he shall receive of mine, and shall shew it unto you" (John 16:14). In John 17:20–22, after he finished praying for the apostles, Jesus said:

> Neither pray I for these alone, but for them also which shall believe on me through their word; That they all may be one; as thou, Father, art in me, and I in thee, that they also may be one in us: that the world may believe that thou hast sent me. And the glory which thou gavest me I have given them; that they may be one, even as we are one.

Taken in context, this is a promise made by the Son of God to all those throughout history who have faith in Him. Many of us may have great achievements on our resume, with tremendous personal wealth and the prestige of men.

Perhaps we have great ambitions, dreams, and desires, or have seen awesome and wonderful sights that transcended our imaginations. Presumably none of us, however, have seen or experienced anything that approaches the glory of God. Jesus makes an unbreakable promise to us that He will share that glory with us through eternity. Other false religions and cults make claims to their followers about what to expect, but all fall short of the promise by the living God to share His glorious presence with us.

Holy Spirit Baptism

Christians can and should stake a claim to this promised offer from Jesus to receive His glory. "There is one body, and one Spirit, even as ye are called in one hope of your calling; One Lord, one faith, one baptism, One God and Father of all, who is above all, and through all, and in you all" (Eph. 4:4–6). This is not a debate about free will or election. This promise is available to anyone who wants it. It has to be appropriated by every individual, but Jesus will not reject someone who believes in Him.

"For the kingdom of God is not in word, but in power" (1 Cor. 4:20). That power is the mind of Christ through baptism in the Holy Spirit. Let's get something out of the way right now. I know I am baptized in the Holy Spirit because the Bible tells me so, and that is all the assurance required. I have not, however, as others have reported, experienced any electrical tingling sensations in the limbs of my body. I don't speak in tongues, but if I wanted to fool you into thinking I did I could probably pull it off. Jesus has never appeared to me like a ghostly apparition or in any other form for that matter. I have not experienced any strange numbness, no levitation, no being slain in the spirit or falling over backwards, no trances or unusual spiritual voices, no beautifully radiant supernatural lights, and no rushing winds from heaven. I have never seen an angel, good or bad, never seen a miracle, never had a supernatural vision, and have never been overcome in any way, shape, or form by a spirit of any kind. The thing I experience most often from God is a well-deserved kick in the seat of the pants, figuratively, more often than not.

Other people may have experienced supernatural baptism in the Holy Spirit, and that is fine. Maybe some day I will too, and that would be very nice. In the interim, I am not going to fiddle around waiting to stake a claim to the promises Jesus makes in the Bible, and neither should anyone else. After His resurrection the Lord said to Thomas, "Because thou hast seen me, thou hast believed: blessed are they that have not seen, and yet have believed" (John 20:29). Jesus is talking about me here, because I haven't seen Him, yet I believe. That promise belongs to me, the blessing is mine, and no one is going to talk me out of it because I haven't experienced the same thing they claim to experience.

It isn't necessarily prudent for Christians to compare someone else's experience to their own. It may be interesting or edifying, but the "whole armour of God" Paul talks about in Ephesians 6:11–17 isn't stamped out on an assembly line so that it only comes in one size. It would be a dirty trick for God to promise us armour that didn't fit or wasn't real. We would show up on the battlefield with the "helmet of salvation" on our head and find out it is a dunce cap, and reach down to pull out our "sword of the Spirit, which is the word of God," (Eph. 6:17) and find a party favor in our hand. That isn't how the almighty God does business.

What Jesus says in Ephesians about the armour of God,

through the apostle Paul, is truth Christians can stake their life on. In addition to the "helmet of salvation" and the "sword of the Spirit," the whole armour includes the:

> …loins girt about with truth, and having on the breastplate of righteousness; And your feet shod with the preparation of the gospel of peace; Above all, taking the shield of faith, wherewith ye shall be able to quench all the fiery darts of the wicked.
> —Ephesians 14–16

It may be that this faith healer over here and that evangelist over there are more baptized in the Holy Spirit and fear God more than I do. Praise God and glory to Jesus, good for them. I am just thankful for what God sees fit to give me and can't worry about what He has given another. We are reminded of the parable Jesus told in Matthew 20, when the man hired laborers to work his vineyard. He paid those who had worked since early in the day exactly what he promised them, but he was generous as well by paying those he had hired late in the day the same amount. When those who had worked since early in the day complained, the man asked, "Is it not lawful for me to do what I will with mine own? Is thine eye evil, because I am good?" (Matt. 20:15). Rather than worry what God has given to someone else, I am going into the dressing room to suit up the armour God has set aside for me, and if you're smart you will, too.

Amazing Grace

We should "fear, lest, a promise being left us of entering into his rest, any of you should seem to come short of it" (Heb. 4:1). We should not fear that we haven't been baptized in the Holy Spirit because we don't deserve it or because we are just miserable low-down sinners. Although it is true that we don't deserve it and we are miserable low-down sinners, so is everyone else and God graciously blesses us anyway. If being perfect were a prerequisite to Holy Spirit baptism no one would have it.

We can be fairly certain, however, that due to the power of words, if someone says there is no such thing as baptism in the Holy Spirit, God will agree with them. God can be very agreeable in giving people what they speak. You may remember the twelve spies in Numbers 13 and 14 who scouted out the Promised Land before the children of Israel. Ten of them said they couldn't possess the Promised Land because the inhabitants were too strong. God agreed with them, but He also agreed with Joshua and Caleb, who said they could possess the land with the Lord's help. Unfortunately, the ten who brought back a negative report caused the rest of the people to err, and Israel wandered in the desert for forty years as a result. People who say the Holy Spirit isn't real speak the truth only so far as it pertains to their own lives.

Mechanics of the Spirit and Soul

> For the word of God is quick, and powerful, and sharper than any twoedged sword, piercing even to the dividing asunder of soul and spirit, and of the joints and marrow, and is a discerner of the thoughts and intents of the heart.
>
> —Hebrews 4:12

The Bible doesn't give a precise definition of soul. We know Jesus has a soul because He said so. "Now is my soul troubled; and what shall I say? Father, save me from this hour: but for this cause came I unto this hour" (John 12:27). Hebrews 4:12 describes the Word of God as alive and powerful, like a razor sharp sword that cuts so cleanly and deeply that it creates a division between the soul and spirit. The sword is double-edged so it cuts both ways. The analogy used is of a separation between the skeletal joints that knit and fit our body together, and the marrow in our bones, which produces the blood that gives life.

"For the life of the flesh is in the blood: and I have given it to you upon the altar to make an atonement for your souls: for it is the blood that maketh an atonement for the soul" (Lev. 17:11). We may notice here that blood atones for the soul, not the spirit. In Leviticus 23:27–32, the Lord speaks about the day of atonement as a time for the children of Israel to afflict their souls, not the spirit.

The same thing regarding atonement is true of redemption. The soul is redeemed in the Bible, never the spirit. For example, Psalm 49:15 states, "But God will redeem my soul from the power of the grave: for he shall receive me." Psalm 69:18: "Draw nigh unto my soul, and redeem it: deliver me because of mine enemies." Psalm 72:14: "He shall redeem their soul from deceit and violence: and precious shall their blood be in his sight." Atonement can be made for the soul, and the soul can be redeemed, but neither applies to the spirit.

Paul used skeletal joints as analogies in Ephesians 4:16 and Colossians 2:19. "From whom the whole body fitly joined together and compacted by that which every joint supplieth, according to the effectual working in the measure of every part" (Eph. 4:16). "And not holding the Head, from which all the body by joints and bands having nourishment ministered, and knit together" (Col. 2:19). He described the joints as knitting or holding believers together in the body of Christ. The blood gives life to the soul, and the Holy Spirit knits and joins together individual souls into the body of Christ.

A person can have a functional soul, and the Spirit of God may provide the life force necessary to motorize the body, but it is the Holy Spirit that stitches the person into the body of Christ. According to Hebrews 4:12 the Word of God judges the thoughts and intents of the heart. It lays bare all our wickedness, pride, hateful anger, and evil imagination and exposes our soul to piercing light. Our emotions, vanities, and motivations are revealed, and we see our reflections in the mirror that is the Word of God. When we see our image reflected back through the Word of God we see ourselves as God sees us.

We must ask Jesus for the Comforter, the Holy Spirit, to dwell with us and regenerate us with the mind of Christ. The Lord won't give the Holy Spirit to one of us because he is more deserving, and withhold Him from the other person because he is less deserving. We are both equally undeserving. It is only through the amazing grace of God that He gives us anything at all instead of what we deserve, that is, eternal damnation. Because Jesus has redeemed our souls through His shed blood, the Holy Spirit will knit with our spirit, and bring us together with other believers into the body of Christ.

A PRIZE OF GREAT VALUE

Whatever that spiritual life force or energy is that motorizes our body, we know it can be separated from our soul. In Revelation 6:9, as the fifth seal is opened, John writes "I saw under the altar the souls of them that were slain for the word of God, and for the testimony which they held." These souls were separate from their bodies but continued to exist. Whether that bodily energy is part and parcel of the Holy Spirit, or another spirit of God apart from the Holy Spirit, is unknown. This is speculative, but perhaps it is the Spirit of Christ, who "is before all things, and by him [Jesus] all things consist" (Col. 1:17). Whether this motorizing force is part of the soul, or different between humans and animals, or whether animals even have souls, is unknown.

One thing seems certain, however. Whatever that motorizing force is, God places an extremely high value on it. We may surmise this is true based on many verses in the Bible where God warns us not to mistreat animals. Of particular note is a verse in Deuteronomy 22 where Moses is giving instructions to the children of Israel shortly before his death. Moses tells them what to do in the event they come across a bird's nest with eggs in it. "But thou shalt in any wise let the dam go, and take the young to thee; that it may be well with thee, and that thou mayest prolong thy days" (Deut. 22:7). In other words, it is all right to eat the eggs, but the mother bird was to be set free. This would allow her to have eggs at another time and continue the species, as well as that particular bird family. They weren't allowed to wipe out an entire bird family, the mother and her chicks, all at once.

What is most interesting about this verse is the part that says, "that it may be well with thee, and that thou mayest prolong thy days" by following God's instructions regarding the bird's nest. These words are almost identical to the ones God used when giving the children of Israel the fifth commandment in Deuteronomy 5:16. He says, "Honour thy father and thy mother, as the LORD thy God hath commanded thee; that thy days may be prolonged, and that it may go well with thee, in the land which the LORD thy God giveth thee." The same promise of prolonged days and well-being is given for sparing the life of a bird, as for honoring one's father and mother. We may conclude the fear of God encompasses even the treatment of little birds. "The fear of the LORD prolongeth days: but the years of the wicked shall be shortened" (Prov. 10:27).

The point here is not to diminish the importance of a person's father or mother. Rather, it is to elevate in importance the spirit, or motorizing energy, that God has given to that bird. Before Jesus completed His work on the cross the sacrificial system was still in effect. Animals served as substitutes for people, and were killed in sacrifice to atone for sin. The death and spilled blood of a goat or bull may or may not hold much importance to us, but God certainly places a high value on it, and that is significantly more important than what we may think.

When Jesus was a little baby, His parents brought Him to Jerusalem, "to offer a sacrifice according to that which is said in the law of the Lord, A pair of turtledoves, or two young pigeons" (Luke 2:24). I don't think it's improper to suggest God placed more value on those two turtledoves that were sacrificed than He places on all the gold and diamonds that have ever been found on planet earth. The life of two little birds is more important to God than all the riches and glory that man has been struggling and fighting over for thousands of years. If two birds are that important to God, imagine how much more important we are to Him. That is why Jesus said, "Even the very hairs of your head are all numbered. Fear not therefore: ye are of more value than many sparrows" (Luke 12:7).

If we are to have the mind of Christ and the fear of God, we must conform our mind to His on the things that are important. Gold is only valuable because people say it is, not because God says so. In Revelation 21, the new Jerusalem comes down from heaven "and the city was pure gold" (v. 18), as well as the street (v. 21). These verses may be figurative, or God may literally want everything made of gold.

I suspect they may be figurative, with a spiritual value far greater than the element we call gold represents.

God places a tremendous value on the spirit that He has given us. We may sometimes get down and feel less than important or think someone else isn't very important, but that isn't the way God views things. We may rest assured God did not invest us with His Spirit because He wanted us to fall short of the promises He has made. We can also be certain we weren't given this most precious of gifts because He wanted us to be defeated by unnatural fears. He gave us His Spirit fully equipped and outfitted with the necessary tools to overcome every mountain and every fear that lies before us. The only thing that can cause us to fall short is failing to have full trust and confidence in Christ.

CHAPTER 16

THE MOTHER OF ALL FEARS

> For the wrath of God is revealed from heaven against all ungodliness and unrighteousness of men, who hold the truth in unrighteousness; Because that which may be known of God is manifest in them; for God hath shewed it unto them.
>
> —ROMANS 1:18–19

C. S. LEWIS wrote in *The Great Divorce* that "There are only two kinds of people in the end: those who say to God, 'Thy will be done,' and those to whom God says, in the end, 'Thy will be done'"[1] Those who fall in the first category are saved and will go to heaven while those in the second category are unsaved and will go to the lake of fire. The people who are going to suffer eternal torment will do so because that's their choice.

The Lord is "not willing that any should perish, but that all should come to repentance" (2 Pet. 3:9). Paraphrasing Charles Spurgeon, we should never discuss the subject of eternal torment without having tears in our eyes. Every cognizant, rational human being who has ever lived or who ever will live has contemplated the implications of an omniscient, omnipotent, omnipresent, eternal God.

> The word of God is quick, and powerful, and sharper than any twoedged sword, piercing even to the dividing asunder of soul and spirit, and of the joints and marrow, and is a discerner of the thoughts and intents of the heart. Neither is there any creature that is not manifest in his sight.
>
> —Hebrews 4:12–13

Unfortunately, we are not all children of God. "He that is not with me is against me: and he that gathereth not with me scattereth" (Luke 11:23). "Ye are of your father the devil, and the lusts of your father ye will do. He was a murderer from the beginning, and abode not in the truth, because there is no truth in him" (John 8:44). Jesus Christ spoke these words, and they don't leave any room for an ambivalent or disinterested third alternative.

The Fear of Eternal Torment

If God defines the fear of the Lord for us as "hatred of evil," what are we to make of someone who denies that evil exists? It is probably a safe bet they aren't God-fearing and, unless they change, most likely have an appointment with the lake of fire. Evil is a reality because God says it is, and we can confirm the truth of what He says with our eyes. Because God is holy, He will not coexist with evil throughout eternity. If eternal evil is to exist God has designated a place for it in His creation, a quarantine area if you will, that is determinate.

I for one am grateful this is the case. Looking at the world we live in, I am convinced that almighty Creator God can do better than this. In fact, He did do better than this until mankind came along and botched things up. God can't be expected to tolerate idolatry, murder, terrorism, war, abortion, school massacres, hatred, racism, and a host of other evils created jointly by Satan and man. He wouldn't be much of a God if He were willing to tolerate these things through eternity. God asked the nation of Israel, "Is my hand shortened at all, that it cannot redeem? or have I no power to deliver?" (Isa. 50:2). God doesn't have a short hand, and He doesn't have a short arm. There are no limits to what He can do. But He isn't a tyrant, and if some folks don't want to join Him in heaven He isn't going to force them to. He also isn't going to force those who do have faith in Him to spend eternity with those who don't because that would be an eternal nightmare.

The concept of eternal torment is a bitter pill for some folks to swallow. We may take comfort, however, from the thief on the cross in Luke 23. He was saved at the last possible moment, and his hands that were nailed to that cross never came together again while he was alive for work in service to the Lord.

I have heard Christians who had dedicated most of their lives to the Lord say that didn't quite seem fair. Again, we are reminded of the parable Jesus told in Matthew 20 about the workers in the vineyard. Some worked all day, some worked several hours, and some only worked an hour, but they all got paid the same. Those who had worked the longest complained because they didn't receive more, even though they received exactly what they had initially agreed upon. The good man of the house asked, "Is it not lawful for me to do what I will with mine own? Is thine eye evil, because I am good?" (Matt. 20:15). Eternal salvation is the Lord's to give, and we should be grateful He makes it so easily available to all of us. Our prayer should be that every thief on every cross receives it.

THE MANNER
AND METHOD OF DEATH

There are very few people who look forward to death. Certainly no one who fears the true living God is looking forward to death, and rightly so. Death is a result of the curse God warned Adam of regarding the tree of the knowledge of good and evil. "Thou shalt not eat of it: for in the day that thou eatest thereof thou shalt surely die" (Gen. 2:17). It seems reasonable to conclude that most people without faith in Christ probably have greater trepidation regarding their pending death than those with faith in Christ. There is also a seemingly small, and one would pray finite, minority that openly embraces the curse of death. Islamic terrorists who measure their righteousness by the sum total of victims innocently murdered are a prime example of twisted and tortured souls who have mined the depths of human depravity. One can only assume the Lord will judge them most severely.

But for those who do fear God and believe He is who He says He is, our faith should ease our trepidation toward death. In fact, it is fair to hold fast the belief that our death should not be our worst day but our best, although certainly not in the same context as an Islamic suicide bomber. There is no reason for Christians to be cynical about it; rather, we have reason to hope our death will be similar to that of Moses. "Moses was an hundred and twenty years old when he died: his eye was not dim, nor his natural force abated" (Deut. 34:7). We may not live 120 years, but there is no reason not to be full of vigor and strength when the Lord takes us.

If we are otherwise, there may be a lesson God wants us to learn from a slower, more debilitating process. In view of the many people who die without Christ as Savior, it may be that a deliberate and more painful wind-down leading to death is a last attempt by God to persuade some to lean on His everlasting, eternal arms. A painful death is well worth the price if it results in a saving, last-minute turn to Christ in faith. Perhaps the agony of crucifixion was the only thing that could move the thief on the cross to repentance at the last moment.

It may be there is a lesson someone else needs to learn from the manner in which we die, gracefully or otherwise. Many great saints of God throughout history have gone through a tough, unpleasant, and painful process of dying, passing on great faith and strength to those they leave behind. Christ on the cross does not stand alone in that regard. Jesus is the foundation of our faith, but some of the bricks that foundation supports include the apostles Paul and Peter, as well as John the Baptist, Stephen, and other martyrs who died ugly deaths that strengthened those who followed.

None of us know what goes on in a person in the final hours or moments before death, particularly when an individual has suffered an extended illness. We all know stories, and perhaps know someone who was aware of their pending death in the hours preceding it. My father-in-law, who was quite a rascal himself, announced saving faith in Christ before his death. He had suffered a long illness and would probably fit the "thief on the cross" category. He didn't wait until the very last second, but he didn't leave a whole lot of time to spare, either. We weren't there when he passed away, but that morning he calmly had his sons carry him downstairs to the living room because he wanted to say goodbye to everyone. He made a few phone calls to relatives to wish them well. His sons carried him back upstairs to bed and he died shortly afterwards, and by all reports he was at peace with himself and God.

No Fear

No one is certain what was going through his mind in those last few hours except for him and God. We don't know how he knew he was going to die at that time or what it was that made him so calm. We had known he was dying for several weeks, and our prayers were that when the Lord took him it would be a soft landing. Our prayers were answered.

A gentle departure is what we should expect from God when we die, and if it is otherwise we must be prepared to complete whatever purpose He has set before us. On 9/11/01 passengers on a hijacked aircraft forced it down into a Pennsylvania field before it could reach its target and kill countless additional innocent people. By all accounts, those who helped bring that plane down were God-fearing Christians. Their act of heroism took supernatural strength and courage that could only have come from Jesus Christ.

As Stephen was being stoned in Acts 7, "He, being full of the Holy Ghost, looked up steadfastly into heaven, and saw the glory of God, and Jesus standing on the right hand of God, And said, Behold, I see the heavens opened, and the Son of man standing on the right hand of God" (v. 55–56). We don't know if the passengers on that aircraft saw something similar that gave them the courage to perform their deadly task, or if they were turbocharged with strength and conviction from the Holy Spirit, or both. We do know their actions had an absolute and certain outcome, and that the love of Jesus Christ provided an override of their fear of death. "Greater love hath no man than this, that a man lay down his life for his friends" (John 15:13). There is usually not much glory in death, but those passengers died in service and in glory to God. We should humbly pray that our deaths should similarly serve the glory of God like those of the passengers on United Airlines Flight 93.

CHAPTER 17

FEAR OF THE BIBLE

All scripture is given by inspiration of God,
and is profitable for doctrine, for reproof, for
correction, for instruction in righteousness.
                                    —2 TIMOTHY 3:16

ERE IS A word you may have never heard before. The word is *perspicuous*. It may be defined as something that is easily understood or readily apparent. If we apply this definition of *perspicuous* to the Word of God it would mean the Bible is clear and understandable on basic as well as essential matters. We can also stretch the definition of *perspicuity* to mean a person reading the Bible today would be able to grasp the author's intended core message, and that the interpretation is the same today as it was one thousand years ago. What this means in practical terms is that none of us should ever be afraid that if we read the Bible for ourselves we won't be able to understand it.

No Fear

For centuries people have pressed the notion that the Bible is not perspicuous. They have said the Bible can only be understood in the original language, and that spiritual value is lost in the translation. Some Jews make that claim about the Hebrew scriptures, and Catholics defended the Latin translation for the same reason. In fact, there are Christians today who even make the claim that the King James English version is the only legitimate translation. The idea that God can only communicate with absolute precision in one language or translation runs counter to the concept that the Lord "is longsuffering to us-ward, not willing that any should perish, but that all should come to repentance" (2 Pet. 3:9). It makes more sense that manipulative leaders would discourage people from exploring Scripture on their own in order to retain power, than to believe that God would select only one effective language for transmitting His Word. It seems reasonable that God can communicate effectively in any and all languages in any and all eras of His choosing.

The debate over which translation of the Bible is best is, for the most part, obtuse. There are plenty of good translations and for the most part there isn't a dime's worth of difference between them. Having said that, beware of the Watchtower Bible and Tract Society (Jehovah's Witnesses) New World Translation. If a person is concerned about the legitimacy of a translation, they can get a Revised Standard, a New King James Version, and a New International Version and compare them. Most of them have footnotes that offer alternate translations on verses that are contentious, so it isn't as though they are trying to dupe anyone.

God isn't trying to be sneaky, or to make the plan of salvation so complicated only a professional class of priest, pastor, or theologian can understand it. If He had wanted to

150

make it difficult for us, why would He have done all that hard work Himself on the cross? Jesus has done every bit of work necessary for our salvation, and the only thing we have to do is believe Him. He isn't asking us to run a mile in under four minutes, bench press 500 pounds, or hold our breaths underwater for ten minutes. "But the anointing which ye have received of him abideth in you, and ye need not that any man teach you: but as the same anointing teacheth you of all things, and is truth, and is no lie, and even as it hath taught you, ye shall abide in him" (1 John 2:27).

PRESSURE FROM WITHOUT

In some circles, "fundamental Christian conservative" or "fundamental evangelical Christian" is a profanity. Our reaction to that kind of thinking should be a stifled yawn or, for those requiring a more outgoing display of disapproval, an emphatic shrug of the shoulders. We don't need to fear what people think of us if we boldly state we believe the Bible is the inerrant, infallible Word of God. If we don't have faith in Christ and the Bible, the only alternative is to have faith in our self-righteousness. Although unbelievers will deny being self-righteous, without a standard for truth beside themselves, what other alternative is there?

There is a sharp line of contrast between those who love and fear God and those who don't. People who are antagonistic to the faith try to blur the line by incorrectly defining the debate in terms of a shallow mischaracterization of the Bible and the gospel message. For example, since it is acceptable to ignore certain portions of the Mosaic Law, such as stoning adulterers, then obviously portions of the Bible are no longer relevant to modern society. God must therefore approve of certain rule changes to accommodate the advance of modern culture and ideas. That makes sense because, after all, things have changed and people are different today than they were 3,000 years ago. The Bible is a good book, and there is much that can be learned from it, but only as a rough guideline, and certainly not as something that can be strictly adhered to. "Eye for eye, tooth for tooth" (Exod. 21:24) is out, Jesus Christ is in, and for the most part, as long as no one gets hurt, anything goes.

This line of reasoning is based on false premises, and allows the Bible to be set aside as the standard of truth. It is a deliberate misrepresentation and confusion of the gospel message of Jesus Christ, in context with the Old Testament and the dispensation of law. It is also based on the faulty premise that God has changed, and man has changed, when in fact neither has changed. Although it can sometimes be difficult, it is the responsibility of Christians to understand and reconcile the dispensation of law with the dispensation of grace. The adversary wants to misrepresent God's ordered plan of salvation. He blurs the line between man's self-righteous failure to obey the whole law, and man's success in obeying the whole law through faith and the righteousness and grace that is of Jesus Christ.

We will always remain in a defensive posture if we allow the foundational elements of God's plan, which is the gospel, to be misrepresented. We must never fear going on the offense to boldly defend the Bible against insincere and malevolent slander.

There are few unbelievers with the courage to boldly state their belief that the Bible is a fairy tale from start to finish, so they resort to more subtle methods to try and discredit it. In their cynical denial of the inerrant truth of the Bible, they would leave man adrift from God with no hope for salvation, no standard of truth, no chance for fellowship, and no Savior.

If faith in Christ and the inerrancy of the Bible makes us dimwitted rubes that is a very small price to pay. "Whosoever therefore shall confess me before men, him will I confess also before my Father which is in heaven. But whosoever shall deny me before men, him will I also deny before my Father which is in heaven" (Matt. 10:32–33). Our greatest fear should be that we would ever deny Christ as our Savior.

MASTER THE WORD OF GOD

This may be somewhat controversial, but the opinion offered here is that no one will ever slay all the dragons of fear and overcome all mountains in their life without constant immersion in the Bible. The Bible is easily available for review and study to all of us. There is no excuse for all Christians not to be well versed in all sixty-six books of the Bible. Paraphrasing Daniel Webster, he said that no man's education is complete until he has read the Bible. We might add "thoroughly studied" to this paraphrase of Webster.

Certainly some aspects of the Bible are difficult to understand. That should not discourage us; rather, it should challenge us. Unlike the comic strips or the sports pages in the local newspaper, it is God's intent that His Word challenges us. When we reach a puzzling section of the Bible, God intends us to meditate on it and try to work through its meaning. We should chew on difficult passages like a dog chewing on a bone. When we have chewed on it so all the marrow and juicy flavor is gone, and we still haven't figured it out, we should just drop it and keep moving along in our Bible study. Difficult passages are one of the things that make the Word of God as wonderful as it is because they give us food for our minds. They keep us questioning and curious, with a desire to always learn more. We may not solve a difficult passage this time, but we may gain new insight the next time.

Difficult passages can instill in us a sense of wonder. For example, I have never been able to fully understand why God gave us the story in Joshua 15:17–19 about Caleb giving his daughter springs of water. Caleb "gave her the upper springs, and the nether springs" (Josh. 15:19). Not only are we given this story in Joshua, God repeats it in Judges 1:15. I have heard some pretty weak explanations about why these springs are important, but none of them has the full ring of truth to them. Maybe those springs are still prominent somewhere in Israel today, or maybe they will be prominent in the future. The fullness of meaning of this story just remains elusive to me.

Ezekiel's temple, starting in Chapter 40 of his book, is one of the most contentious and puzzling mysteries of the Bible. Although some folks claim to have all the answers, most explanations fall short after some last, desperate leaping conclusion that is necessary to tie everything up in one neat package. The animal sacrifices that are supposed to take place in that temple also defy an easy explanation, but Christians should find meditating on the meaning of that more interesting than meditating on *Sports Illustrated*. The fact that we don't understand every aspect of the Bible should be no cause for discouragement, rather it should serve as a source of challenge.

If we use the parent-child analogy again, every parent expects their child to listen when they are providing instruction for the child's benefit. Too many of us don't listen to God when He provides us instruction through His Word.

The actual percentage of the Bible that is consumed by genealogies, laws for cleansing of leprosy, and instructions for animal sacrifices is miniscule. We shouldn't use that as an excuse to deter us from a full and scholarly understanding of its contents. Neither should we let the cynical beliefs of unbelievers deter us from acknowledging that the Bible is as it claims to be, the Word of God. There is no better way to master our fears than by mastering the Word of God, and obtaining an in-depth knowledge of its contents should be singularly the highest priority in our lives. It will turn the mountains in our lives into molehills and give us a lifetime of priceless meditations on the things of Jesus Christ.

CHAPTER 18

THE FRUITS OF THE FEAR OF GOD

THE FEAR OF the LORD is to hate evil. It is the beginning of wisdom and knowledge. Knowledge of the holy God gives us good understanding, that we do His commandments and depart from evil. Fear the LORD for our good always that He may preserve us alive, give us strong confidence and a place of refuge, that we will be satisfied and without want, and not visited with evil. (Paraphrase of Proverbs 1:7; 8:13; 9:10; 14:16; 19:23; Job 28:28; Deuteronomy 6:24; Psalm 34:9; 111:10).

The fear of the Lord is defined in numerous verses throughout the Bible. The paraphrase above, discussed earlier, contains many of the fruits of the fear of God, but it seems worthwhile at this point to provide a more complete listing. There are many verses, and referencing them all seems a bit unnecessary. But in order to gain a full appreciation for the benefits of the fear of God additional discussion is provided.

Wisdom, knowledge, and understanding are fruits that help us in our relationship with a holy God. These gifts aren't automatically developed with experience or age, and are not the products of hard work and discipline. They result from a life dedicated to the service of God, and concern the things of God and holy living. They do not necessarily concern the things of the world. For example, in the parable of the unjust steward, Jesus said that "the children of this world are in their generation wiser than the children of light" (Luke 16:8). We may interpret this to mean that those who are concerned only with the flesh are wiser than Christians in obtaining the things of the flesh. Concerning the wisdom of God, however, we may note that it is eternal. In referring to wisdom we read, "The LORD possessed me in the beginning of his way, before his works of old. I was set up from everlasting, from the beginning, or ever the earth was" (Prov. 8:22–23). The eternal value of God's wisdom certainly exceeds anything that may be gained by the wisdom of the flesh.

Additional fruits of the fear of God include a prolonging of days, a place of refuge, and it provides us with a fountain of life. These three fruits alone should do much to alleviate our unnatural worldly fears, because with Jesus Christ as our fountain of life God expects us to enjoy secure and extended life spans.

The fear of God also brings riches, honor, and praise that are more valuable than the great treasures of the world. We receive the additional fruits of happiness, uprightness, strong confidence, satisfaction, and we won't be visited with evil. With these wonderful gifts from God, there clearly is no room for the unnatural fears of the world, and no place at all for dread fear.

WHAT DOES THIS FRUIT LOOK LIKE?

For who hath known the mind of the Lord, that he may instruct him? But we have the mind of Christ.
—1 CORINTHIANS 2:16

With the mind of Christ and the fear of God, the priorities of a Christian will be significantly different than those of the world. Would you rather have all the gold in Fort Knox, or be in the will of God and receive His blessing for your life, whatever that might be? That is an easy question for believers and nonbelievers alike to answer, but the answer is different in both cases.

"For since the beginning of the world men have not heard, nor perceived by the ear, neither hath the eye seen, O God, beside thee, what he hath prepared for him that waiteth for him" (Isa. 64:4). The apostle Paul said essentially the same as Isaiah in 1 Corinthians 2:9, that it has not "entered into the heart of man, the things which God hath prepared for them that love him." It is beyond our greatest imaginations what God has waiting for those who put their trust and faith in Him. We can no more imagine what to expect than we could count all the grains of sand on all the beaches in the world. We might get some idea of what to expect from the Garden of Eden before the fall, but even that comes short of what is ahead. That is why Christians should be filled with hope and joy and optimism every single day, not just once in a while on rare occasions. "Be thou in the fear of the LORD all the day long" (Prov. 23:17). Our attitude of looking forward in glorious anticipation should be the rule, not the exception.

No Fear

This is true of our daily lives now, and it will be true in eternity. We will be blessed in our present lives if we fear God and if we possess the spiritual discernment to recognize a blessing when it comes our way. Our minds are like radio receivers: first the switch has to be thrown to the "on" position, and then the dial tuned to the right frequency. No matter how many stations are broadcasting, if the receiver is turned off we are not going to hear anything. If the receiver is turned on but tuned out, we are only going to get static. Our brains have to be turned on through the Word of God to the mind of Christ, and we have to tune them in through the fear of God to recognize the blessings He sends us.

What do these blessings look like? "For who hath despised the day of small things?" (Zech. 4:10). That is a question God asked Zerubbabel after the Babylonian exile, during the building of the second temple. Zerubbabel had laid the foundation for the temple, and God was reassuring him that his hands would finish the task. Building a temple is like a lot of other things. It is one small thing after the next, one stone after another, a little mortar, smoothing, more mortar, smoothing, another stone, layer by layer. A Christian's life should be the same way. If you take a lot of good little things and add them all together, after a while they amount to a very great thing.

We could change Zechariah 4:10 to read, "For who hath despised the day of small blessings from God?" and it would mean almost the same thing. The smallest of blessings might include that energy of spirit that causes our heart to expand and contract to circulate blood, and the exchange of carbon dioxide for oxygen in our lungs, a force of energy no one can explain. God could snuff out that energy at His pleasure, and we would stop breathing and return to dust. It is a blessing that the Creator of the Universe would care

160

enough about you and me to feed and shelter us, and invest us with His Spirit. It is a blessing that we have easy access to His Word, and we are free to worship Him without persecution. Good health is a blessing if we have it, and chances are that won't always be the case. Because Christian's aren't conformed to the world, we appreciate these blessings from God that unbelievers take for granted.

Typically, blessings are very small; that is how it works. Some people seem to expect enormous blessings on a routine basis. Today I win the lotto, tomorrow I get discovered for a big part in a Hollywood movie, the next day I meet the girl of my dreams, the following day I strike oil in my back yard, and the day after that it's a vein of gold in the front yard. Shazam, praise the Lord!

God doesn't part the Red Sea, raise the dead, or send fire down from heaven every day of the week, and anyone who expects that is going to face disappointment. He doesn't think like we do, and His priorities are different than ours. What type of blessings should we expect from a God who places more value on the life of a sparrow than He places on all the gold and diamonds in the world combined? If you answered small blessings, you would be right. We have to understand and agree with God that if a blessing is important to Him it probably isn't small at all. He just tells us that so we know what to look for and can recognize it. Some people tune their receivers to a frequency that will only receive the enormous blessings, and they tune out all the little ones. When the big ones don't come they think they are getting cheated, but they have cheated themselves out of the ones that are important to God. Christians must calibrate their minds through the fear of the Lord to recognize what is important to God, and to receive those things gratefully and with humility. To be in the will of God means we have aligned the priorities in our lives with His. By this we are in position to be of service to Him and receive His blessings.

Small blessings can be a kind word from a stranger, or making a good impression on a new business contact that can lead to increased opportunities years later. It can be playing with a kitten and a string, or watching lilies come to life after a long winter. A blessing may be a small favor you do for someone else, one you don't even think is worth mentioning, that returns to you one-hundred-fold some time later. It can be a Bible verse that comes to mind in a moment of stress, providing a calming influence and refuge from anxiety. It could be a twenty dollar donation you made to a preacher getting turned into a bus ticket for an old woman that gets her home, and you don't even know about it. A small blessing may be a good meal, a warm fire on the hearth on a cold night, a good night's sleep, or a quiet moment when you realize by intuition that you are in the will of God.

Many people miss the opportunities God sets before them because they fail to recognize blessings that are right under their noses. It would seem a self-evident truth that before large blessings can be enjoyed, we must first learn how to appreciate the small ones. If someone can't appreciate a good home-cooked meal, how can they appreciate one cooked at the finest restaurant in Beverly Hills? If a person hasn't learned to appreciate a beautiful sunset today, why would they appreciate it more if they watched it from a beachfront house in Malibu tomorrow? If someone can't enjoy a single rose, how can they enjoy the millions of roses in the Tournament of Roses Parade in Pasadena, California, on New Year's Day? If I give you my last dollar and the shirt off my back, and you don't appreciate it, you will never appreciate it if I give you a million dollars and a brand new wardrobe. A person who can't recognize and be grateful for the smallest blessings can never be grateful for the largest ones.

A SPIRITUAL REPORT CARD

The Holy Spirit provides us with the capability to perform critical self-evaluation. Do we love and fear God, and keep His commandments? As Christians, we should already know the answer to that question. We shouldn't need God to hand us a report card like a little child because we should already know what our grades are. Are we lazy and disinterested in the things of God and about life in general? Have we thought about Jesus in the last ten minutes, or the last hour, or the last ten hours, or the last ten days? As we reflect on our day was it one filled with evil imaginations, impatience, and anger? Or was it a typical joyous, meaningful, and pleasant day filled with numerous small blessings and accomplishments, with wondrous meditations on and about the Lord? Are we patient and calm? Are we not caught up with the cares of the world, but quietly and steadily forging ahead with Jesus Christ at our side? This should be the expectation of those who fear God.

"The heart of the righteous studieth to answer: but the mouth of the wicked poureth out evil things" (Prov. 15:28). The apostle Paul told us much the same in 2 Timothy 2:15 when he wrote, "Study to shew thyself approved unto God, a workman that needeth not to be ashamed, rightly dividing the word of truth." As Christians, we should know if we have studied the Bible to the approval of God. If we aren't comfortable with the Bible it should come as no surprise that we aren't enjoying the full blessings of God. Paul used the words "study" and "workman" in 2 Timothy 2:15. We don't need to look those words up in a concordance, and

163

we don't need to pray for spiritual discernment or baptism in the Holy Spirit to properly interpret what He means by "study" and "work." What we might want to pray for is that Jesus would make this particular "study" and "work" a labor of love, which He will do.

We may not win the national spelling bee or revise Einstein's set of gravitational field equations, but there is certainly no reason for a Christian to have to suffer being a dimwit. God will provide us with the brainpower we need to perform any task He sets before us. If we look to Jesus and seek His direction, He will give us the tools we need to be successful. He will make us as intelligent for a task as He wants us to be, and certainly we will be smarter with Him as opposed to without Him.

"To the weak became I as weak, that I might gain the weak: I am made all things to all men, that I might by all means save some" (1 Cor. 9:22). Paul says, "All things to all men." Please be indulgent as I take the liberty to substitute some words in this verse, appealing to the mind of Christ that is in us. We might say, "To the strong became I as strong, that I might gain the strong." "To the gentle became I as gentle, that I might gain the gentle." Perhaps we can stretch this verse a little further without torturing it. "To the angry became I as soothing, that I might gain the angry." "To the hard of heart became I as tender of heart, that I might gain the hard of heart." "To the selfish became I as generous, that I might gain the selfish." Although these verses lack inspiration, they seem to fall under Paul's canopy of "all things to all men."

The operative point is that Christians possess far more ability and the capability for critical self-assessment than we give ourselves credit for. This is due to the fear of God, the mind of Christ, and the indwelling presence of the Holy

Spirit. Christ possesses unlimited resources and places them at our disposal as the need arises, provided we fear God and operate within His will. He is the One who makes us "all things to all men" in order to accomplish His will through the Christian believer. He outfits us with the skills and gifts we need to witness effectively, the armor we need to do battle, and the temperament and discernment to handle difficult circumstances with grace and humility. With the fear of God as our strong foundation we can approach each new and challenging situation in our lives with a spirit of truth, confidence, and sound judgment.

CHAPTER 19

WHAT'S THE DIFFERENCE?

And be not conformed to this world: but be ye transformed by the renewing of your mind, that ye may prove what is that good, and acceptable, and perfect, will of God.

—ROMANS 12:2

WHAT SHOULD BE different about God-fearing Christians, as opposed to those who are either ambivalent or have rejected Jesus Christ? Should there be any evidence in a Christian's life that we are filled with God's spirit and separated to the Lord? Would we be found guilty in a court of law of being a Christian? If we can't answer these questions with specificity then it is likely our walk in the Spirit and our life in Christ are empty platitudes and the fear of God a cliché.

Our faith does not depend on someone else's definition of it. Some may rail against the Christian belief in the Trinity but that does not make us idolaters. We were created in God's image but there is much about Him we don't understand, and that shouldn't be a cause for concern or apology. Christians worship God the Father, God the Son, and God the Holy Spirit, and He is one God. "For my thoughts are not your thoughts, neither are your ways my ways, saith the LORD. For as the heavens are higher than the earth, so are my ways higher than your ways, and my thoughts than your thoughts" (Isa. 55:8–9). We may not fully understand the Trinity but neither do we fully understand why a larger mass produces greater gravity than a smaller mass. It is nonetheless true.

Christians rely on the Bible as a baseline reference or standard against which we measure where behavior falls in relation to the sovereign will of God. We hold the Bible as the prism through which we view the world and as the basis for the judgments we form, and we aren't ashamed or fearful to do so. We lean on the righteousness of Christ, not our own. We don't spend a lot of time worrying about what others do and we don't go on search-and-destroy missions to root out sin in the lives of others.

Christians have reverence and respect for God's creation. We expect our children to live happy, healthy, and productive lives learning worldly skills in school and spiritual skills at home and at church. Our children don't engage in riotous and violent demonstrations, cheer the death of the innocent, or act as ammunition runners in the midst of terrorist gun battles. They are protected and cherished, not manipulated like political poker chips or aborted before given an opportunity to serve God. Our children are taught to fear God, not the world.

Christians are appreciative of God's blessings, like the fruitful and productive earth He has given us, recognizing it is temporal. The earth is a blessing God has provided that we must care for, but He has also given us dominion over it for prudent and guiltless exploitation. We aren't unwelcome intruders on God's planet, and we don't measure our righteousness by how many of His generous gifts we reject.

THE FEAR OF GOD AND AMERICA

The primary tool of warfare for Christians is the Word of God, not guns and bullets. We seek to make it available to all without restrictions on race, nationality, or ethnicity. We make no claims that only a people of one language can receive its blessings, but that all nations and all peoples may learn to fear God for eternal salvation and life. Our God is all-powerful and doesn't need to ration out blessings lest there be a shortage. Any who look to Him can receive abundant blessings with assurance they are not at the expense of someone else. We serve God by our witness and encourage others to choose a personal relationship with Christ. We recognize that the decision they ultimately make is not dependent on us, but rests entirely between them and God.

Second to Christ, we love and respect our country, not because it is perfect but because, God willing, we will be a beacon of light and truth to the world. We seek not to export our less endearing tendencies but our generous ones, first and foremost which is the love of Christ and His gospel. We hope to share His blessings with others, not deprive them from those less fortunate. We look to lead others not because of what we say, but because of who we are in Christ.

Christians recognize this country is not able to stand between a generous and loving God and someone else upon whom He seeks to pour His blessings, nor should we try to do so. Another nation or group of people who aren't enjoying God's blessings should look to Him for a solution, not us. The United States is the world's lone superpower, but we don't have the strength to stand between God and a nation He has chosen to bless. Neither can we stand between God and a nation that has brought curses upon itself, and force God to pour out blessings anyway. Those who blame us for their ills should perhaps fire their false god and hire the real deal. He works for free.

There should be no guilt among those who seek the face of God and accept His generous blessings just because others do not share our faith. But we should also muster our compassion for those who reject God's blessings and embrace the curses instead. We must not show disdain for those without the fear of God, or for those tortured and lost souls who are unable or unwilling to find room for the Lord in their hearts. It may be difficult to show compassion to those who hate us and are hostile to the things of Christ. But the grim reality of a life without faith and absent hope, while also facing the prospect of eternal separation from God, should be a sober reminder to us of just how high the stakes are and how much they have to lose.

We must be careful not to make the mistake of identifying the "correct" position on political issues as righteousness in the fear of God. We must, however, recognize that it isn't possible to be a Christian while rejecting clear biblical teachings, fundamental truths, and values. Those who would use our faith as a political poker chip by claiming to be Christians, while working to undermine its core values, should be chastised. Jesus never hesitated to openly chastise the self-righteous who claimed to hold faith, yet whose actions betrayed them. "O generation of vipers, how can ye, being evil, speak good things? for out of the abundance of the heart the mouth speaketh" (Matt. 12:34). He didn't care whether He hurt the feelings of the scribes and Pharisees or not and neither should we.

There is a tendency to blur the line between faith in American-style democracy and faith in God, as though the two were equal. Love of country should never equal or replace love of God. "Jesus said unto her, I am the resurrection, and the life: he that believeth in me, though he were dead, yet shall he live: And whosoever liveth and believeth in me shall never die" (John 11:25–26). Individual freedoms, inalienable rights, the pursuit of liberty and happiness, human equality and justice for all are wonderful ambitions. Engaging in the political process to uplift downtrodden, oppressed, and disenfranchised people is also a noble pursuit. A person may even win the Congressional Medal of Honor for heroism in defense of his country, but unless his faith rests in Jesus Christ, he will not be saved. U. S. citizenship doesn't earn a pass at heaven's gate.

Christians need not apologize for being the moral compass of this country. We have faith in God's inerrant Word as a standard of truth. Those without faith have no standard but the one they have self-righteously invented. It is no wonder we are unable to predict the actions of unbelievers. With no common standard, how could we? Their brains are like those lotto machines with the ping-pong balls floating around inside—you never know what number is going to pop out next.

TIME'S-A-WASTING

As individual Christians, we should place a premium on the time God has given us and not worry when our interests diverge from those who lack faith. We should not expect to conform to the world because we carry the sword of the Spirit in our hearts. This gives us grace and power that non-Christians don't have and may lead us to activities they consider less than exciting, uninteresting, or quaint. We don't spend countless stupefied hours comatose before a television set as our life slips through the fingers of our hand that clutches the remote control. Brainless sitcoms, profane reality shows, and nighttime soap operas don't fit in with a spiritual agenda. We know that at this moment Jesus Christ is sitting at the right hand of God to intercede on our behalf. He didn't suffer and die on the cross and ascend to heaven so we could sit around drinking beer and watch people eat insects on *Survivor*. We are free to do that if we choose, but as born-again Christians the spirit in us will probably choose differently. Our affections are "on things above, not on things on the earth" (Col. 3:2).

We don't waste time endlessly surfing the Internet for information that has no edifying value. Doing a word search on the "Blue Letter Bible" Web site is probably worthwhile, logging onto an Internet chat room, probably not. Pornographic Web sites are for those whose soul is deeply troubled. Any professing Christian who visits them has good cause to have a dread fear of God. Remember King Ahab who was killed by an arrow shot out of nowhere for his wickedness? If Christians engage in evil behavior like pornography, they shouldn't be surprised if God pins a bullseye on the back of their shirt like He did to Ahab and then an arrow hits spot-on the center circle.

We understand that God has given us a limited amount of time, and we will fall short of His will and His promises for our lives if we engage in the same meaningless and repugnant activities as unbelievers. Christians are aware of American pop culture, and that it simply doesn't matter. It is vacuous and without substance, driven primarily by advertising revenue and the love of money. It should not concern a Christian or occupy their time any more than is either necessary or unavoidable. It doesn't make any difference whether we are up to speed on the latest trends, or whether people think we are boring, old-fashioned fuddy-duddies. We monitor news and current events but do not allow them to consume us. We look for those things that bring glory to Jesus Christ and avoid those things that don't. We find walking in the spirit with Jesus Christ in the fear of God more rewarding than squandering precious time in pursuit of meaningless entertainment. "Being confident of this very thing, that he which hath begun a good work in you will perform it until the day of Jesus Christ" (Phil. 1:6). We won't perform that good work if we are killing time on trivial activities like box scores, crossword puzzles, and *Wheel of Fortune*. The Holy Spirit will lead us to something more worthwhile, edifying, and eternal if we let Him.

WHAT'S THE EVIDENCE?

As Christians, we know we are different and not conformed to the world, but what is the evidence? There should be something in our lives we can point to and say, "See, this is different. That's one of the things that makes me a Christian." What could that evidence be?

Do you sleep well every night and wake up in the morning looking forward to each new day with a spirit of joy and hope? Do you enjoy each day even if it isn't the weekend and you have to go to work? You are supposed to. Do you generally enjoy your work and recognize how fortunate you are to have employment of some kind? Do you make the most out of your job and do it well? By the time you head out the front door to start your new day have you been appreciative to God for all the blessings He has bestowed on you, like a hot shower and a nutritious breakfast? Are you happy and content? If the answer is no, the solution to the problem rests in Bible study, Jesus Christ, and the fear of God.

No Fear

If our relationship with Jesus is right, we shouldn't have many bad days. We will have bad times, certainly, such as flat tires, stopped up toilets, dogs barking in the middle of the night, and going to the dentist. We still have to take out the trash, wash the dishes, and sweep the garage. But traffic jams and bad haircuts don't ruin our outlook on life. Tragedy will strike on occasion, such as a house burning down or a loved one dying, but those are usually rare occurrences. Jesus will always pick us up from tragedy, set our lives in order, and cause a renewal of faith. Through the fear of God we retain our joy in Christ, and don't become cynical and embittered as the hard knocks of life take their toll.

"And we know that all things work together for good to them that love God, to them who are the called according to his purpose" (Rom. 8:28). Paul doesn't say, "We believe that all things work together for good"; rather, he says, "We know that all things work together for good." The reason we know all things work together for good is because we have seen it happen time after time, day after day, year after year. We have evidence this is a true statement. It might be hard to put that evidence on a scale and weigh it, or stretch out a tape reel and measure it, but it is tangible nonetheless. Deep feelings of love, hope, joy, quiet peace and contentment, patience, and an enthusiasm for living are qualities Christians should constantly experience and be constantly thankful for. This is the rule, not the exception.

A Christian's life should be one filled with constant progress, just like Zerubbabel's temple. Small little changes, small little blessings, day by day, year after year are not to be despised but cherished. They all add up and grow together to form a lifelong commitment to Jesus Christ. Our relationship with the Lord should be in a state of constant renewal, not stagnant or in steady decline. In this regard we know

174

where we stand if we want to. If a person doesn't know it is because they don't want to. It is like when our pants appear to be getting gradually tighter around the waist, there is a reason for that, and we know what it is. A person can go out year after year and keep buying pants with a larger waist size, or they can choose to lose weight. A person can walk away from Jesus or they can choose to walk with Him, but let's not kid ourselves, the choice is ours to make.

CONSTANT RENEWAL OR SAME OLD SAME?

And be renewed in the spirit of your mind; And that ye put on the new man, which after God is created in righteousness and true holiness.
—EPHESIANS 4:23–24

What does it mean for a Christian to be constantly renewed and transformed in spirit of mind? Is that just warm, fuzzy, nebulous religion-speak, or is it something real that produces practical change in our lives? If it isn't real, then the Bible isn't what it claims to be, the Word of God. "Then Peter said unto them, Repent, and be baptized every one of you in the name of Jesus Christ for the remission of sins, and ye shall receive the gift of the Holy Ghost. For the promise is unto you, and to your children, and to all that are afar off, even as many as the Lord our God shall call" (Acts 2:38–39). If these things aren't real, then the Holy Spirit isn't who Paul claimed Him to be in 1 Corinthians 2:12–13: "Now we have received, not the spirit of the world, but the spirit which is of God; that we might know the things that are freely given to us of God. Which things also we speak, not in the words which man's wisdom teacheth, but which the Holy Ghost teacheth; comparing spiritual things with spiritual."

NO FEAR

As Christians we are supposed to "put on the new man" (Eph. 4:24). The new man doesn't walk around with a chip on his shoulder and isn't in a constant state of anger or aggravation. He doesn't suffer from anxiety attacks and doesn't live in dreadful fear that catastrophe is just around the next corner. The new man doesn't spend a lot of time dwelling on doubts and negativity. When he finds himself thinking that way he quickly consults himself in the spirit of his mind and changes the subject to something positive. He doesn't allow his thoughts to linger over unfruitful, negative, self-defeating thoughts. The Holy Spirit gives us power to control the way we think, and the things we think about. We are not animals subject to random sensory inputs and stimuli that control our thought processes. Our spirit and the Holy Spirit control our thought processes, and we determine what it focuses on and the direction it goes in.

Christians should be victorious over sinful and unproductive thoughts such as bigotry, intolerance, racism, sexism, distrust, and meanness. If we walk through life and don't see evidence of these things in the world it is because we are not paying attention. They exist in unfortunate abundance. If we don't pay attention to these ugly sins we will either unknowingly fall victim to them or be victimized. We should not behave as drunkards, liars, sluggards, cheaters, whiners, and complainers. Only on rare occasions should we suffer emotions such as anxiety, depression, fear, anger, jealously, or cynicism, and when we do we should immediately recognize them and cast them away. Our mind is directed either by the Holy Spirit jointly with our soul, or it is not. There will always be momentary lapses, but there is no in-between on who is in charge of our brain. Either we are calling all the shots or the world is.

Christians should be successful in those things they choose to do, as long as they fear God, shun evil, and seek after His will. We should be successful in our work, and we shouldn't live in a constant state of fear that the world will come crashing down around us. We should be optimistic and hopeful for the future. We look to God for help in achieving personal success in our work and don't waste time on get-rich quick schemes. We are thankful for what God has seen fit to give us and don't fret over what He hasn't given us. We look to God for success through prayer, and are always willing to provide the labor, toil, and sweat necessary to accomplish a purpose.

If we are willing to work, God will give us opportunities for success. He wants to give us the material and physical items we need to prosper. He will even give us a little bit extra when necessary to provide blessings to others. If He wants us to share money with someone else He will give us extra money. If He wants us to share something that isn't of a material nature, such as a spirit of joy, hope, and optimism, He will give that to us in abundance

Hidden With Christ in God

Christians should enjoy Bible study because it produces within us spiritual fruit, and prevents us from becoming spiritual nuts. We should not be intimidated by other people, bosses, or coworkers. We don't lack self-confidence and assurance. If we find ourselves in a tough or embarrassing situation with another person, we immediately look in our mind's eye to the Lord for guidance. If someone is being ornery or giving us trouble in some way, the Lord will see us through it. "The fear of man bringeth a snare: but whoso putteth his trust in the LORD shall be safe" (Prov. 29:25). Snares aren't something that generally chase us around, they are something we step in. The Lord has given us the tools we need not to step into the snare of the fear of man.

"For ye are dead, and your life is hid with Christ in God" (Col. 3:3). People see us every day and we see them. But where is our head and where is theirs? If we are stuck in traffic do we curse our bad luck and the guy next to us, or is our mind hidden with Christ in God? Are we upset because we are going to be ten or fifteen minutes late, or are we thankful that Jesus will get us there safely? Where is our head when things don't go quite the way we planned? Do we allow ourselves to get unnecessarily upset, or instead think of Jesus sitting at the right hand of God on His throne, interceding on our behalf?

Christians know the answer to all these questions, but here is the most important one of all. Is there anything more important, day in and day out, than your relationship with Jesus Christ? If you wanted to sum up the difference between a Christian and a non-Christian, that would just about cover it. Only you and Jesus know the answer. We all fall short of the mark, constantly, but Christians never stay there. If you asked a non-Christian what the most important thing in their life was, they would probably struggle for an answer. For a Christian, that should be the easiest question in the world.

CHAPTER 20

OVERCOMING THE WORLD: A RALLY TO FAITH

Who is he that overcometh the world, but he
that believeth that Jesus is the Son of God?

—1 JOHN 5:5

I MAGINE, IF YOU can, an ancient, mysterious castle
nestled on a picturesque mountaintop surrounded
by dense forest, manicured gardens, and rugged out-
croppings of rock. The castle appears dark, foreboding,
and intimidating, silhouetted against the sky as dark storm
clouds gather against the setting sun. It dominates the landscape, like a mighty, impregnable fortress that has stood
since time eternal.

Inside the castle are opulent chambers, luxurious sitting rooms, a massive wood-carved den, elegant dining
areas and long, ornamented passageways. The carpets are
thick and plush, and decorative chandeliers hang from
high, vaulted beams in the ceiling. Beautiful artwork and

embroidery adorn the walls, and every aspect of the interior décor has been finely detailed by master craftsmen and artisans. Priceless stained glass murals line the eaves and frame the breathtaking views of the surrounding forest and mountains from every window.

You discover elaborate false panels and concealed doorways that lead to secret inner chambers and reveal an underground network of tunnels and waterways. Entrance is gained through remote levers and switches cleverly hidden in the nooks and crannies of the woodwork, or disguised as a single thin bookbinder on the voluminous shelves filled with classic first-edition masterpieces of literature. Located in the secret chambers beneath the castle are vast treasures of gold, diamonds, emeralds, rubies, and silver. There are golden chalices, figurines of ivory and silver, sapphire rings, pearl necklaces, jeweled bracelets, chests filled with bullion, priceless pieces of artwork by renowned masters on every wall. The luxurious castle is so imposing and the wealth inside so enormous, a lifetime of exploration wouldn't be enough to discover all its ancient mysteries or find all its hidden treasure.

Our Greatest Treasure

Like the old castle, the Holy Bible is timeless, foreboding, sometimes dark, standing in sharp silhouette as a beacon of truth against a stormy world of fear, hatred, and lies. It has withstood countless assaults from unbelievers of every generation who neither fear God nor shun evil, but as a magnificent fortress, it is impervious to the siege works brought against it. As everything around it withers and decays with age, fading to dust, the Bible dominates the landscape with a view beyond the horizon stretching from the beginning to the end. It was given to mankind as a gift, like an ancient chart mariners would use for navigation, leading not to a new continent but to salvation and eternal life.

The Bible is an elegant and priceless masterpiece with nooks, crannies, crevices, and difficult passages that defy a lifetime of exploration. Sometimes as we search, we become lost, and pray for a guide who will lead us to understanding through the different ages in man's troubled relationship with God. But we never stay lost for very long. The Holy Spirit of God will lead us through complex, maze-like passages that seem to lead from one dead end to another, to secret chambers without outlet and doors that are sealed shut. But when the Spirit pulls the right lever, a new outlet opens into a wide passage filled with brilliant light and increased understanding. "Ye need not that any man teach you: but as the same anointing teacheth you of all things, and is truth, and is no lie, and even as it hath taught you, ye shall abide in him" (1 John 2:27).

Compared to the ancient wisdom and knowledge contained in the Bible, the wonderful treasures of the mysterious old castle wane to insignificance. The castle speaks of fading glory while the Bible speaks of hope eternal. The castle and its art are the work of men's hands, but the Bible is the work of men's hands made perfect by the Spirit of God. "All scripture is given by inspiration of God, and is profitable for doctrine, for reproof, for correction, for instruction in righteousness" (2 Tim. 3:16).

Do you know of anyone who has spent a considerable amount of time and effort studying the books of the Bible with an open heart, who doesn't believe it? Have you ever met someone who approached the Bible in faith, and after a diligent search of its nooks and crannies, walked away disappointed with what he found? Can you think of a person with a genuine, transforming love for the Word of God who has permanently turned his back on it? I can't think of anyone who fits any of these descriptions. Do you think a person who has committed his heart and soul to seeking the face of the Lord, searching through all the cracks and crevices of the Bible, would trade what he has found for anything in the old castle, or for the entire castle itself?

The Fear of Falling from Grace

"Howbeit, because by this deed thou hast given great occasion to the enemies of the LORD to blaspheme" (2 Sam. 12:14). This was part of Nathan the prophet's rebuke to King David for killing Uriah the Hittite and taking his wife. Christians today give the enemies of the Lord opportunity to blaspheme His name when our behavior is abominable. There are some who suggest it isn't possible for a born-again Christian to fall out of God's grace, and that doing so is an indication they were never true believers in Jesus to begin with. That may or may not be true, but we certainly know King David fell out of God's grace, although it wasn't permanent. Even though David sinned, there is no indication his heart was ever turned away from God. His son, Solomon, on the other hand, fell out of God's grace "because his heart was turned from the LORD God of Israel" (1 Kings 11:9), but presumably that was not permanent. David and Solomon serve as strong warnings to Christians that we are never immune from a sudden and catastrophic falling-out of God's will.

When Christians commit egregious sins, damage is done to the body of Christ. That damage, however, shouldn't necessarily have an effect on the faith of individual believers within the body. Our faith should not waver one millimeter when someone else falls short of the glory of God. When we fall short of God's glory or are challenged with adversity, He expects us to use that to strengthen our faith and grow in Christ. When clergy or other Christians engage in financial, sexual, or other improprieties, they disgrace only themselves and will have to answer to the Lord Jesus Christ. The more severe damage is done to those outside the body of Christ who are discouraged from entering into fellowship as believers in Jesus. These failures serve as excuses for "scoffers, walking after their own lusts" (2 Peter 3:3) to profanely blaspheme the keeping power of God.

BACKING OFF

"Blessed is the man that walketh not in the counsel of the ungodly, nor standeth in the way of sinners, nor sitteth in the seat of the scornful" (Ps. 1:1) Psalm 1:1 lists three things we shouldn't do, while Psalm 5:8 gives us help in accomplishing them so we can receive the promised blessings: "Lead me, O LORD, in thy righteousness because of mine enemies; make thy way straight before my face." It is the Lord's righteousness and His straight way before us that will lead to His blessings. When the enemies of the body of Christ heap derision and scorn on the body itself because of the members that may have fallen, it is not necessarily our task to either join in condemnation or rush to anyone's defense. There is no commandment saying we are required to have opinions on every controversial matter of religious faith, or on the status of the eternal soul of another.

It may be that all that is expected from God-fearing Christians is to simply learn from failure, "For godly sorrow worketh repentance to salvation not to be repented of" (2 Cor. 7:10). Unbelievers view failure as an opportunity to capitalize on someone else's weakness or to slander the Christian faith. They fail to recognize that confession of sinful mistakes and whole-hearted repentance brings believers into closer fellowship with God. Ungodly sinners vehemently criticize believers who, during the course of seeking God, predictably fall short. They are called hypocrites for following after the righteousness of God, and then not measuring up to the perfection of Jesus Christ. Many unbelievers are unable or unwilling to recognize the difference between a hypocrite and a repentant sinner.

When an unbeliever follows his own self-righteousness it is hard for him to fail because he is usually able to meet his own low standards. If he does happen to fail, he can always revise his standards downward, making them less demanding and success more probable the next time around. Christians have to follow the standard of Jesus Christ, so the demands become greater and the failures more evident as we progress in our walk with the Lord.

Digging In

Implicit in the admonition of Psalm 1:1 to not stand in the way of sinners, however, is the concept that we shouldn't spend a lot of our time worrying about their sins. Most of us have enough of our own without fussing over someone else's. It is ironic that an unbeliever will accuse a Christian of being self-righteous, when we know we don't have any righteousness of our own. Then they will fret that we want to impose our religious beliefs and standards on them, when Psalm 1:1 tells us not to worry excessively about what they do. We certainly shouldn't hold the door open for them as they commit their sins, but we shouldn't try to padlock it shut on them either.

Part of being a Christian is showing tolerance. God is tolerant and longsuffering, and if a person is determined to go to the lake of fire for eternal torment, He won't stand in their way. We should follow God's example, but we do have the responsibility to warn sinners what the outcome of their behavior will be. God told the prophet Ezekiel what the duties of the watchmen were. "If when he seeth the sword come upon the land, he blow the trumpet, and warn the people; Then whosoever heareth the sound of the trumpet, and taketh not warning; if the sword come, and take him away, his blood shall be upon his own head" (Ezek. 33:3–4). It is the duty of Christians to blow the trumpet and warn the people. We must never fear being watchmen in the tradition of Ezekiel. God told the prophet, "As an adamant harder than flint have I made thy forehead: fear them not, neither be dismayed at their looks, though they be a rebellious house" (Ezek. 3:9). If we fail to act as watchmen the blood of sinners will be on our heads, and it won't wash out any more than Jesus' did off the hands of Pontius Pilate. That will require us at times to be hardheaded like Ezekiel, and we may even have to bang heads with unbelievers on occasion.

"To every thing there is a season, and a time to every purpose under the heaven" (Eccles. 3:1). There is a time to back off on the defense of the faith, and there is a time to dig in and fight to the last man. If we take "the sword of the Spirit, which is the word of God" (Eph. 6:17), what should we do with it? What is a sword used for? It is sharpened on the edge so the task of cleaving through fibrous tissue can be done efficiently, and it has a point that can pierce through clothing, leather, or layers of vulnerable outer defense. A real sword is used for stabbing into and through flesh, for cutting and dismembering human appendages. A sword pierces vital organs, veins and arteries, causing substantial bleeding, inflicting severe pain, and inducing trauma. It slices through muscle tissue and tendons, incapacitating an enemy so mobility is lost, and eventually the ability to offer a strong defense is lost.

A sword is something that has to be picked up and held in our hands. As we become familiar with it and practice its use, we will become more proficient, increasing our chances of survival in battle. A sword serves a dual purpose in warfare, and those who resolve to use it only in defense assure their own defeat. A sword used in offense, on the other hand, can be used to deliver a killing blow, but the option to show restraint is also available. No one has exercised more restraint in His dealings with fallen mankind than God. He has given us the sword that is His Word because He trusts we will use it wisely. We should use it on offense to bring glory to the name of Jesus Christ and not faint at its first use when it draws fresh blood from our enemies. In the end, "The dust shall return to the earth as it was: and the spirit shall return unto God who gave it" (Eccles. 12:7). The Lord Jesus will then take the measure of us, to judge whether we have used His sword with mercy, in accordance with His righteousness and in the fear of God.

EPILOGUE

THE BIBLE IS the standard by which Christians measure the world. Our race or ethnicity, income, or education level, nationality, sex, strengths, and weaknesses don't matter when we meet together on the common ground that is the Word of God. God gave the Bible to fallen mankind in order to open our hearts to His offer of eternal loving-kindness, and it is tragic so few have responded to His generosity. He gave us His Word to slay our fears, not add to them.

There are many who criticize Christians for accepting the gracious offer of eternal love and fellowship with Jesus Christ on His terms. Some reject His divine offer out of hand without listening to a proposal that costs them nothing. They will have an opportunity to press the terms of their demands on God before the great white throne. If some of them are able to persuade the Lord and change His mind, that is fine with me. That is between them and Jesus, and in the spirit of love I wish them well. Before that happens, may the Lord provide us wisdom for an effective witness of faith in hopes that some won't have to appear before that throne. If we can't persuade them to hear the Lord's proposal, may He give us the grace to hold our peace, shrug our shoulders, and walk away without looking back. We may leave behind some whom we love, but in order to avoid the same fate as Lot's wife we have to continue looking forward.

Unbelievers get angry with Christians for what we believe. If we hold the belief that "there is none other name under heaven given among men, whereby we must be saved" (Acts 4:12), and those who don't believe are destined for eternal torment, some people get very upset. They don't think it is fair, and it makes them mad. But Jesus hasn't authorized us to get mad at them for what they believe because He gave them the freedom to make that choice, and it isn't ours to take away. It might be nice if they would extend us the same courtesy, but don't expect it. Many of those who think it is acceptable to reject Jesus fail to appreciate the irony of a situation where it is fine for them to be mad about what we believe, but we are not supposed to be mad about what they believe. But that is the way the Lord would have it, and as Christians He holds us to that higher standard.

Unbelievers also fail to appreciate the irony of a God who is infinitely more loving, kind, merciful, compassionate, and generous than we are, who would actually have a place reserved in His creation for those who choose eternal torment. When people do something wrong, for example, murder each other, we usually put them in jail and may in fact execute them. Even if they apologize, we will probably carry out the sentence on them. Of course, we have no way of seeing inside their heart to see if they really mean it when they say they are sorry.

Because God is infinitely greater than we are, He does things differently. If we murder someone, or commit adultery, and later turn to Him in repentance from the depths of our soul, He will look inside our heart to see if we really mean it. If He sees that we would rather die than offend Him again in that way, God not only forgives us but He doesn't even remember our sin (Isa. 43:25). He understands we are all going to make mistakes. All He expects is for us to apologize and mean it, and to agree with Him regarding right and wrong. Apparently that is asking too much from some people. They think they are smarter than God, and their foolish pride makes them believe they are better at defining right and wrong than He is. They gripe and moan about how mean and harsh God is because He won't surrender His sovereignty into their hands.

Jesus hasn't authorized us to change His plan of salvation or His Word as it is contained in the Bible. In fact, nowhere are we given authority to apologize for Jesus, His plan of salvation, or His Bible, and neither has He offered an apology Himself. If anyone expects us to apologize for God, we must without fear decline to do so in a spirit of humility. Neither has Jesus authorized us to impose our biblical worldview or our faith on others. From Genesis 1:1, all the way through to Revelation 22:21, and every single verse in between, there is nothing that tells us we must try and force anyone to believe as we do.

Neither has Jesus required us to justify His position to anyone. He has not told us we are to use our own skills of persuasive logic and self-righteousness to convict some-one of sin who is in rebellion against Him. Through the Holy Spirit He will give us the gentle humility of spirit to act as a watchman without anger or malice. In fact, He may even give us the grace to let a person who is in open rebellion have the last word of an argument, and allow us to meekly disengage from the debate without losing a moment's peace. If the last word with us is something they prize we might as well let them have it. That is all they will win, because they won't have the last word with the Lord.

Christians have no need to fear falling short of God's plan for our life, and our joy in Christ is not dependent on the grace of those who choose to reject His call. God intends us to slay all dragons and overcome every mountain in our life. When we fear God, no one has power to stand between Christ and us, and no one has the strength to block the blessings He intends to pour out on us. "Because greater is he that is in you, than he that is in the world" (1 John 4:4). Elisha said much the same when he was surrounded by the host of the Syrian army and God delivered him. "Fear not: for they that be with us are more than they that be with them" (2 Kings 6:16).

God's Spirit places a call of truth to every human soul, and each soul is responsible for the answer it gives. "Behold, I stand at the door, and knock: if any man hear my voice, and open the door, I will come in to him, and will sup with him, and he with me" (Rev. 3:20). God is the only One who possesses an infinite capacity for love. It is also worth remembering that while on the cross, His suf-fering was infinitely greater than anything we can begin to imagine or appreciate. For those who have a difficult time reconciling the concept of eternal torment with a

God who is all-merciful, they must recognize that Jesus has already shed His blood and paid the price of redemption none of us could afford. No one has ever suffered anguish comparable to that of Jesus on the cross for the combined sins of fallen mankind. Only Jesus Christ could bear the additional agony of judging the lost souls at the great white throne who refused to answer His call.

NOTES

CHAPTER 5
THE SCHOOL OF HARD KNOCKS:
EXAMPLE OF THE PATRIARCHS

1. Paul L. Maier, *Josephus, The Essential Works: Jewish Antiquities* (Grand Rapids, MI: Kregel Publications, 1988), 28.

CHAPTER 9
CHAOS AND BRAZILIAN BUTTERFLIES

1. David Wilkinson, *God, Time & Stephen Hawking: An Exploration Into Origins* (UK: Monarch Books, 2001), 68–70.

CHAPTER 16
THE MOTHER OF ALL FEARS

1. C. S. Lewis, *The Great Divorce*, (New York: Collier Books, 1946), 72.

TO CONTACT THE AUTHOR

E-mail: RDByland@jps.net